T0279379

PENGUIN BOOKS

THE GUMPTION OF MR TOILET

Widely known as Mr Toilet, Jack Sim broke the global taboo around toilets and sanitation. He founded the World Toilet Organization (WTO), a global non-profit working towards a world with clean, safe toilets and sanitation for everyone, everywhere, at all times. Born in a slum in Singapore in 1957, he learned entrepreneurship and gumption from his uneducated mother who started a series of small businesses. He was also inspired by the gumption of Prime Minister Lee Kuan Yew and grew up watching the amazing transformation of his country from Third World to First. From a school failure, he became a serial commercial businessman (sixteen businesses). After attaining financial independence he left the rat race to become a serial social entrepreneur. After fighting the bureaucrats, he enrolled at Lee Kuan Yew School of Public Policy and graduated with a Master's in Public Administration at the age of fifty-six. He also graduated at Singularity University's Global Solutions Program at age fifty-nine. Some of the awards he won are: Schwab Fellow of the World Economic Forum, Ashoka Global Fellow, Queen Elizabeth's Commonwealth Points of Light Award, Clinton Global Initiatives Fellow, *Time* Magazine's Heroes of the Environment for 2008. For his contribution to humanity, he received an Honorary Doctorate from the University of Strathclyde, Glasgow, UK, in 2022, and another Honorary Doctorate from Shobhit University in 2024.

the state of our public toilets had much room for improvement. Hence, quirky as Jack Sim's focus on toilets may be, I encouraged him to pursue his passion. Modern sanitation and clean toilets make for a healthier world.

His book, written in a down-to-earth style, captures his *ikigai*. One may not agree with all his views, and the way he pushes them, but his determination to live out his *ikigai* holds lessons on how we can find our own purpose and meaning in life.

—Goh Chok Tong, Emeritus Senior Minister,
Prime Minister of Singapore (1990–2004)

PRAISE FOR JACK SIM

'Jack has started a global clean toilet movement that help governments to shape sanitation policies. One success story is that the World Toilet Organization assisted the Chinese government in adopting the standards for lavatories before the Beijing Olympics last year.'

—Tech In Asia, 30 Jun 2009

'Jack wants to talk about toilet first and himself later, only if needed (more about Jack and WTO in the end).'

—*YourStory*, 15 Oct 2013

'The 56-year-old Singaporean Chinese has become something of a celebrity, helping to break the taboo about talking about toilets, feces, disease and public health.'

—*ShanghaiDaily.com*, 7 Jul 2013

'Jack Sim, the founder of World Toilet Day, travels the world promoting access to safe and clean toilets.'

—*NPR*, 19 Nov 2014

'Toilet man put S'pore on the world map by taking everyone's sh*t seriously.'

—Mothership, 19 Nov 2017

'He's known for his campaigns to tackle the world's sanitation problems.'

—CNA, 22 Jun 2019

'. . . this Singaporean activist encourages communities to build toilets, a product that almost half the world lacks access to.'

—*The New York Times*, 21 Nov 2019

'Shedding a light on this basic human right—breaking stigma and taboos along the way—is Jack Sim's happy crusade, a crucial campaign powered by a wardrobe of costumes ranging from Game of Thrones to Super Mario and loads of poop-themed gags.'

—*Forbes*, 15 Nov 2019

'Jack Sim might shock people, but he's raising awareness about sanitation issues on a global scale.'

—*The Wrap*, 7 Nov 2019

'Entrepreneur Jack Sim put his successful career in Singapore behind him and founded the global non-profit World Toilet Organization (WTO) in 2001. Sim wanted to improve toilet and sanitation.'

—Global Citizen, 5 Nov 2019

'Sim called for a comprehensive behavioural change strategy to focus on transforming mindsets of people and also provide sustainable solutions for easy access.'

—*The Statesman*, 15 Jun 2019

'After traveling the world for more than two decades seeking to improve access to bathrooms, "Mr Toilet" Jack Sim has now plunged into the cinematic world with a film about his unusual campaign.'

—*Taipei Times*, 30 Apr 2019

'Look at the poor as customers who will get attracted to good-looking products. People complain that cell phones are expensive. But do they stop buying them? Toilets too should be made desirable.'

—*The Sunday Guardian*, 20 Nov 2016

'Twenty years after leaving a career in construction to devote his time and energy to humanitarian work, and decades away from the kampung boy who didn't have a toilet, Mr Sim has certainly come far. He continues to travel the world promoting sanitation, and other issues such as good nutrition and poverty alleviation.'

—Asian Scientist, 24 Jun 2019

'His obsession with toilets has had him mingling with presidents, A-list celebrities, he's even had a resolution passed at the UN. After growing up without a working toilet in Singapore he's now on a global mission to make sure others don't go through the same.'

—BBC, 05 Aug 2020

'Raising toilet culture worldwide is top of mind for Jack Sim who looks to solve the global sanitisation crisis with toilet humour.'

—Tatler, 11 Dec 2020

THE GUMPTION OF MR TOILET

MOBILIZING THE WORLD TO EFFECT CHANGE

Jack Sim

PENGUIN BOOKS

An imprint of Penguin Random House

PENGUIN BOOKS

Penguin Books is part of the Penguin Random House group of companies
whose addresses can be found at global.penguinrandomhouse.com

Published by Penguin Random House SEA Pte Ltd
40 Penjuru Lane, #03-12, Block 2
Singapore 609216

First published in Penguin Books by Penguin Random House SEA 2024

ISBN 9789815144802

Typeset in Adobe Caslon Pro by MAP Systems, Bengaluru, India

www.penguin.sg

*I dedicate this book to my beautiful wife, Julie;
my four children, Faith, Truth, Worth, and Earth;
my brother, William; my sister, Sylvia; and my late mother,
Tan Siam Kheng, and late father, Sim Lian How.*

*And to all the readers who are doing their
part to make a better world.*

'The real currency of life is time,
When time runs out, life runs out.
Fame, Power and Fortune become illusions.
What is left behind is not your name but your legacy of goodness.'

'Think like a child, implement like a mother. All problems become simpler and clearer, and you become mission-driven.'

Contents

Becoming Mr Toilet

Successes, Failures, and Works in Progress

Going Beyond the WTO

Foreword

George Yeo

I am conflicted by Jack Sim. I really don't want to get too close to him because I end up being sucked into his vortex. Yet, my conscience does not allow me to turn away because Jack's causes are good causes.

This book by Jack appears to be all about Jack and may initially turn some readers off. But it is much more than that. It is about passion. Without passion, no great projects can be undertaken. Gumption (a word that Lee Kuan Yew popularized in Singapore) is needed and Jack sees himself as a personification of it. From a young age, Jack threw away his comb since he did not think it should matter how he looks. He proclaims himself to have ADHD (which I think is over-rated as a diagnosis). In my occasional frustration with Jack, I try to figure him out. Yes, he is egoistic but he suppresses his small ego to concentrate on his big ego, which are his passions in life. Sometimes I think that there is a little bit of Jack in all of us except that, in him, it is writ large.

In his inimitable way, Jack has moved the world's needle, which very few of us can hope to do in our lifetime, even those with bountiful resources. Better known as Mr Toilet, he has helped to change the world for the better in matters of public sanitation. I know women are particularly grateful to him. In a conversation with a woman in a Third World country some years ago, she lamented how those of her gender deliberately drank less water to avoid having to use toilets. In India and China, better public toilets have improved the lives of hundreds of millions.

Everywhere in the world, we talk about ESG. Yet there is nothing as simple and as important as having better public toilets in many countries. There is frequent market failure in the provision of better public toilets because decision-makers are often themselves not affected. Leadership—moral leadership—is key in this area as in many others. Jack leads the charge and won't readily take 'no' for an answer. I could not say 'no' to him and agreed to be a keynote speaker for a World Toilet Summit in Haikou in 2011. I provided a plank for him to the United Nations (UN) where, with the support of our able (but initially sceptical) diplomats, 19 November was declared as the UN World Toilet Day unanimously by the UN General Assembly. He thanks me publicly but it is for us to thank him.

This interesting book is about Jack and his causes. He wants to be a child again. He counts the days to his expected expiry date. There is much to admire in his approach to life. In his desire to do good, he is more spiritual than he makes himself out to be. We can't all be like Jack and we don't want too many people to be like him, but we should be inspired by his lifework. He says that his only intimate friend is his wife, Julie. But he has many good friends and I am fortunate to be one of them.

At three years old, Jack Sim learned to squat

Introduction

I was born in Lorong Ong Lye, a small, poor *kampong* (village) in Singapore that had only one common row of toilet huts. There was no flushing toilet. It was a row of huts each with a British Bucket below. A truck would come and collect the buckets every couple of days. Meanwhile, visiting the toilet, with large, shiny-green house flies flying all over, was a traumatic experience for a child. Like every other kid, I often suffered from intestinal worms due to our poor hygiene conditions. Our toilet paper was actually old newspapers torn into squares and hooked by a wire.

I remember my brother telling me that when he grows up, he'd not like to be a politician because his face will appear in newspapers and people might wipe their shit on his face. Humour always prevailed in our family—although we were poor, we were a happy family.

Our laughter has continued throughout our lives, and I realized that happiness was not a result of having money. Our happiness was influenced by the stories we told ourselves that shaped our paradigms of who we were and what we wanted to be. In this book, I want to help you learn how to tell yourself stories that could possibly be helpful to you, to reframe your perspectives towards happiness.

My father used to warn me: 'If you don't do well in school, you might become a *jamban* man! [a derogatory term for the

workers who collected shit buckets in the village] Toilet man.'
Unfortunately, I did badly in school, and actually became a
toilet man, not by design but by chance through a series of
unplanned events.

My journeys were journeys of contradictions: from
poverty to financial independence; from high school failure
to professorship, from commercial entrepreneur to social
entrepreneur; and from despising bureaucracy to influencing
policy changes. I'd like to retire from the limelight to focus on
romancing my wife for the time I have remaining on this earth,
which is perhaps not very long going forward.

I wrote this book with the hope that some of these lessons
could be useful to each of my readers. I am confident that these
stories will resonate with your experiences as you see yourself
in them. I've tried to take complex issues and simplify them
into narratives, retelling them as practical life hacks instead of
profound philosophies of perfection, which, to me, are unusable.

I hope these ideas will provoke new thoughts in you. I invite
you to disagree with my thoughts so that you may invent new
solutions for yourself.

Above all, I want your time invested in reading this book to
be enjoyable and give you something in return. Time is a most
precious commodity, because when time runs out, life runs out.
My motto is: 'To live a useful life.'

Open defaecation, a common practice for farmers in India

Self-portrait in 1988

Breaking a Taboo

In human history, many taboos have been broken by revolutions to bring forth a better world.

Slavery was considered a norm until it was not.

Women were confined until the Women's Liberation Movement.

Black segregation took almost a century of legal fights to end in the United States.

Apartheid was unchallenged in South Africa, until it became untenable.

The #MeToo Movement arose when people started to speak up.

All these taboos were considered acceptable norms, until someone said it was unacceptable, and led a movement to change it.

Toilet was one of the last taboos, until we began our campaign in 2001.

Prior to 2001, the words 'toilet', 'sanitation', 'shit', 'pee', and 'poo' were considered rude and unspeakable. Polite society avoided such terms and discussing this topic often led to embarrassment. Academic publications used technical terms like 'faecal sludge management', which is unsuitable for mass media engagement. The neglect of this important agenda led to 2.6 billion people (40 per cent of the world's population in 2000)[1] without access to proper sanitation and 2 million diarrhoea deaths annually.

Unable to sit by and accept this profoundly shocking state of affairs, I broke this taboo through the creation of the World Toilet Organization (WTO) in 2001. With our unique blend of humour and facts, the WTO called a spade a spade and took the global media by storm advocating for better toilets, sanitation, and hygiene conditions for people all over the world.

In 2007, sanitation was voted the most important medical milestone in 150 years by the *British Medical Journal*[2] because it added 20 years to human lifespan. It was rated even more important than antibiotics, anaesthesia, vaccines, and the discovery of DNA structures. This shows that prevention against diseases is the best way to improve public health rather than waiting for people to become sick and then curing them.

May I add that the dignity of having a clean toilet made available whenever needed, is priceless.

Yet, the situation was indeed horrendous. A 2012 Lancet report showed that diarrhoea kills more children under five than malaria, measles, and HIV/AIDS combined.[3] Young girls are dropping out of school because of the lack of privacy when they menstruate. Girls and women are often molested or raped while defecating in the open. Untreated human excreta contaminate rivers and water sources, killing marine life and spreading diseases. Flies visit the open poop piles and transfer pathogens to food, making the poor sick. Poor women get infections when they use old newspapers, straw, or dirty rags as sanitary napkins, because they cannot afford proper ones.

Here are the challenges we need to address:

1. Traditionally, Sanitation was bundled under the Water Agenda by the UN and the development sector at large, but all funding went to water. Sanitation was literally drowned 'underwater' and it received no attention. We had to give the Sanitation Agenda its own publicity.[4]

2. Sanitation was misunderstood as a supply problem, but a large number of toilets donated were not used as toilets but as storerooms instead. We need a new demand-driven approach creating habit change from open defaecation to using toilets. To change long-standing habits, rational persuasion is not enough. We need to reposition toilets as a status symbol of quality life, and an object of desire. To be successful, sanitation must take centre-stage.

3. We cannot continue to see sanitation as a 'problem'. We must see the lack of toilets as a market opportunity. We must sell toilets to the poor in the villages, the way they sell Louis Vuitton bags to the office workers in the cities.

4. These are urgent and under-served needs that can only be addressed as a global crisis at a billion scale through massive transformative movements instead of piece-meal pilot projects, such as building 1,000 toilets here and there.

5. The Sanitation Agenda competes for attention with other major agendas from climate change to health, disasters, food crisis, energy, and terrorism, etc.

Each of these hot topics struggle for mind space, media attention, and airtime, to be heard and supported.

Since the founding of the UN on 24 October 1945, the first UN Water Conference was held in 1977, and the second one was in 2023. It's appalling to see an important agenda such as Water be made a low priority. But if you think Water has been neglected, you should know that Sanitation is even more neglected. That 2023 UN Water Conference devoted only about 5 per cent of the sessions to Sanitation and Hygiene and less than 1 per cent to Menstrual Health, which is a big taboo as well. We live in a world where agendas are addressed according to their charisma. Corporations love green and blue agendas like Environment, where they can use trees, rivers, coral reefs, pandas, and polar bears in their publicity material. They avoid 'Brown Agendas' like Poop, Diarrhoea, Polluted Rivers, which are equally important.

Therefore, in order to succeed, we have to make sanitation sexy, and we have a secret weapon. Since it is a taboo and has been unspoken for such a long time, it has news potential. We created new narratives that helped the media attract massive readerships and advertising income, and the global media took our stories by storm. As we take charge of the narratives, we command the attention of the world.

The World Toilet Organization was founded on 19 November 2001. Our founding day has since been adopted unanimously by all 193 countries of the UN General Assembly as the official UN World Toilet Day. We broke the taboo on the Sanitation Agenda.

In 2010, the blockbuster film *Harry Potter and the Deathly Hallows* was launched globally and was trending at the fourth position on Twitter (now called X) on 19 November, while World Toilet Day ranked fifth. But Harry Potter invested multimillion dollars in publicity while we did it at zero cost. We saw Justin Bieber was trending at the sixth position and catching up with us. So, we tweeted that 'Justin Bieber is doing worse than Shit'. This single tweet sparked a furore of attacks by Justin Bieber's fans, and it boosted our visibility causing us to trend even higher. Suddenly, a lot more people learned about the existence of World Toilet Day.

This is how guerrilla marketing works. We leverage anything and everything, making the irrelevant become relevant to our mission. There is no such thing as bad publicity with an agenda like Sanitation, which is a taboo itself.

I created the World Toilet Organization with the WTO acronym to play a pun on the World Trade Organization. I was hoping that the WTO would sue me, then I'd be famous. It turns out that they didn't sue me, but we became known as the other WTO forever. Nothing sells like contraband. Either way, I won. Eventually, the journalists started calling me Mr Toilet and that moniker created another intellectual property for us with highly sticky brand equity. The most elegant thing is we achieved all this without paying a cent for media publicity and have never paid marketing dollar in the last twenty-four years. When you have no money, work around it.

The Gandhians said: 'First they ignore you, then they laugh at you, then they fight you, then you win.'

Ten years later, I met Pascal Lamy, the Director-General of the World Trade Organization at the World Economic Forum in 2011 in Jakarta. I introduced myself and he exclaimed with some jest: 'Oh, I know you. Yours is the more important WTO!'

Meeting with Pascal Lamy of WTO, 2011

Lesson:

Life is neither easy nor difficult. Life is either fun or boring. Like playing a game, the higher the degree of difficulty, the more fun it'll be. Easy is boring.

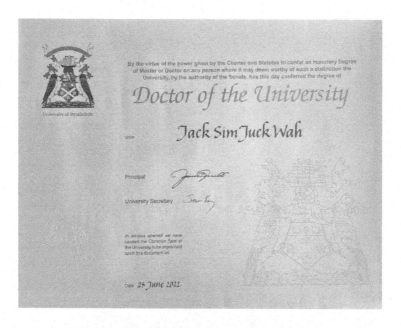

Convocation of Honorary Doctorate in
University of Strathclyde

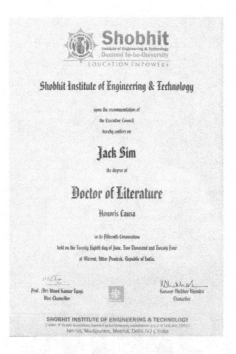

Conferred Honorary Doctorate Degree at
Shobhit University, Meerut, UP, India

Bad Things Can Be Good Things

The good things are good, so I'll just talk about the bad things.

As a child, I was always told by relatives that I was not good-looking. So, I freed myself from trying to look good. I focused on becoming humorous instead.

Growing up, a fortune teller told my mother that according to my palm readings, I will not have any gambling luck. He said I could only rely on hard work to be lucky. This was a good thing and saved me lots of money since I don't buy lottery tickets or visit casinos.

In elementary school, I was often punished for breaking rules and irritating the teachers during lessons. I was sent on stage for public caning by my principal almost every month. That's bad. But I was on stage so often, I've never had any stage-fright since, and that's good.

At sixteen, I failed my high school's O-level examinations and couldn't advance to higher education. That's a bad thing. But that saved me six years of studying and I was able to start working and earning money very early, learning on the job instead, which is a good thing.

I was happy working as a salesman, earning top-dollar commissions, but my good boss was replaced by a nasty boss. That's bad. Thanks to that nasty boss, I resigned from my job and started my own business at the age of twenty-four and grew sixteen profitable businesses. That's good.

My first marriage was a wrong match. I was thirty-one and she was twenty-one. She realized that marriage came too early for her when she was not ready to be a wife. We divorced a year later. That's bad. Three years later, I married Julie. I learned to appreciate a good match, and I'm still crazily in love with her after thirty-three years of marriage and that's a really good thing.

When I was forty, I was quite wealthy, but the Asian Financial Crisis wiped out half of my money. That's a bad thing. My business was doing badly, and many staff members started leaving. A staff member who resigned told me she felt bad for me. She said: 'Unfortunately, bosses can't resign.' I thought over what she said and decided on the contrary that bosses could resign. I decided that I'd bring the company back to health and then retire.

I wanted to quit the stressful rat race. I sold almost all my businesses, bought some houses for rental income and devoted the rest of my life to volunteering for social work. This brought me peace. The joy of serving other people instead of myself was really one of my best decisions.

I saw that 40 per cent of people did not have access to proper sanitation, no toilets or hygiene. Nobody wants to talk about this disgusting subject and 2 million people die of diarrhoea every year. That's a bad thing. I created the World Toilet Organization (WTO) and the UN World Toilet Day, 19 November, and over the last twenty years, our global movement has put the Sanitation Agenda on the media centre stage. Our powerful storytelling drove demand for toilets globally, and incentivized political will to prioritize sanitation to win votes and popularity. WTO has lifted the prominence of the Sanitation Agenda for everyone and, over the last twenty-four years, our global sanitation movement mobilized access to proper sanitation to more than 2.5 billion people in developing countries. It was a very good thing, and it surprises me each day as the global movement continues to grow every day with a life of its own.

My mother often lamented that unlike her siblings' children, none of her three kids made it to university. Even though we were financially successful, I've always felt inadequate as a school failure. So, at fifty-two, I went to the Lee Kuan Yew School of Public Policy and studied part-time for four years. I graduated with a Master's in Public Administration at the age of fifty-six, and am now an adjunct associate professor at the National University of Singapore (NUS).

Graduation at NUS. Master's of Public Administration at
Lee Kuan Yew School of Public Policy 2013

I also enrolled on a Master's of International Marketing course at the University of Strathclyde but failed to finish my dissertation. My professor rejected my dissertation entitled 'Why the world needs a World Toilet Organization'. Even after I demonstrated its success after the launch in 2001, he insisted that I had not backed it up with a robust body of research literature. So, I received a Post Graduate Diploma instead of a Master's degree. I thought that was a bad thing. Twenty years later, in 2022, I was surprised to receive an Honorary Doctorate from the same University of Strathclyde, which is an amazing thing.

Lesson:

The next time you encounter any bad thing, try to see if there is a good thing behind it.

My Mother, Tan Siam Kheng

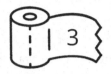

Lessons from My Mother: Necessity Creates an Entrepreneur

I was born in a slum in Singapore in 1957. My father, Sim Lian How, was always wondering how to feed his family. He was a grocery shop assistant, and his meagre salary was hardly enough for three kids, our mother, and our grandmother.

My mother, Tan Siam Kheng, had to think up new ways to raise the income level of our household, as her kids were growing and going to school. Her first venture was making pancakes, which she hoped to sell by piggybacking on our neighbour who peddled fresh fruit from a pushcart. Unfortunately, that neighbour did not promote her pancakes and instead returned all the unsold products in the evening with zero revenue. My mother gave up her first start-up enterprise after three nights of distributing free pancakes to all the neighbours.

After suffering heavy losses from the pancakes, she had only one dollar left. She invested her last remaining dollar in lessons at the community centre, learning how to sew smocking cushions. After the first lesson, she returned home and started teaching six neighbours what she had learned, charging one dollar each for the lesson, thus earning a net profit of five dollars. She used the five dollars to buy yards of cloth, cut them into small pieces and sold them as sewing kits together with needles, thread, buttons, and cotton wool. She became a profitable haberdasher and a teacher!

She invested another dollar for the next lesson of smocking at the community centre and once again taught the same lesson to the six students. But after the fifth lesson, she realized she could develop her own patterns and did not have to attend any more lessons at the community centre. She bought blank square notebooks for ten cents each and made them into pattern books. My brother, sister, and I would hand copy her original designs, reproducing pattern copies for her to sell to her students at two dollars per book. By selling the pattern books, our haberdashery business expanded as more people became keen to make the cushions. This led to my mother selling these cushions to car owners to decorate the back seats of their cars.

The simplicity of her business model was amazing: She had multiple streams of income, from training fees to material sales, to publications, to end product distribution. She not only generated good income for our family, she also created income streams for her students.

Unfortunately, smocking went out of fashion after two years and she had to think of a new business. Mother went to CK Tang (then the biggest shopping centre in Singapore) and saw an opportunity with cosmetics. Eager to sell their products, the cosmetic girls at the make-up counters were looking for would-be customers. She volunteered and allowed them to make her up. As they worked on her face, Mother remembered the whole sequence: from cleansing lotion to foundation, lipstick, mascara, eye shadow, and so on. She bought a full set of cosmetics, went home and tested her skills on my sister's face. She was satisfied with the results. The next morning, she declared herself a wedding beautician.

In 1960s Singapore, the only time a girl had make-up on her face was on her wedding day.

Soon, her wedding beautician business became so popular that on auspicious dates she'd be inundated with bookings. This is how she started a beauty school and began training students. She extended her business to become a one-stop wedding planner with comprehensive services, including masters of ceremony, wedding dinners, photography, bridal gown rentals, flower bouquets, bridal cars, ribbons, and even match-making.

There are two months in the Chinese calendar that are not auspicious for weddings: the month of Chinese New Year and the Month of the Hungry Ghosts. During these months, she focused on matchmaking as an upstream business and when the match was successful, she got paid for match-making as well as managing their weddings. These months were also good for training new students in beauty care. All these supplementary profits she earned became a substantial part of her revenues.

My brother and I helped with procurement. We'd take the bus to Chulia Street downtown to buy cosmetics from the wholesalers, for 30 per cent less than our retail prices. My brother became entrepreneurial and he created another supplementary business. He bought big tubs of Nivea cream at three dollars each, repacked it into six smaller capsules, and sold them under the brand name Pearl Cream at three dollars each. That's a 500 per cent profit over the cost of goods sold. As my mother couldn't read, write, nor understand mathematics, my brother became the bookkeeper.

Throughout her career, she trained about fifty students and created jobs for them. While many worked for her as freelancers, others became competitors. Although there was a feeling of betrayal, Mom taught us that it was better not to bad-mouth one's competitors so as to conserve energy to focus on our own business. I learned very early from her that competitors are a normal part of any business and there is nothing to be upset about. Afterall, it is natural for her students to aspire to be like her.

In cases where customers could not afford to pay, she often helped them out for free. She also donated generously to many relatives who were facing financial difficulties. I learned that charity and business can go hand in hand.

She became the most popular low-cost beautician in Singapore over the next twenty-five years, helping over three thousand brides prepare for their wedding day. At six years old, I was actually attending 'Mother's Business School'. Later in adulthood, my brother, William, and I started a series of sixteen profitable businesses together despite the fact that both of us failed badly in our secondary school examinations.

My mother was illiterate, but she showed me that an academic education is not necessary to start a business. What is needed is gumption. She created a sustainable social enterprise even before the term was invented. She demonstrated that common sense, seizing opportunities, and maintaining a good reputation are the essentials for continuous success.

Our family moved out of poverty, but this was only one of the many stories of how Singaporeans built a nation of entrepreneurs. Our nation of about 2 million people (then) grew up from hardship and we learned how to improve the quality of lives with our own hard work, without relying on others.

At the national level, I grew up watching how our late Prime Minister Lee Kuan Yew and other first-generation leaders transformed Singapore from poverty into one of the wealthiest nations in the world based on the same philosophy of hard work, self-reliance, and personal initiative. Our GDP was USD 500 per capita when we gained independence from Malaysia in 1965. In 2023, it was USD 88,000, one of the highest in the world.

In 1978, China's supremo Deng Xiaoping visited Singapore and adopted our economic model of entrepreneurship. He returned to China to implement his 'Open Door Policy' for international investments. By 2023, his market-oriented reforms lifted more than 800 million Chinese people out of poverty, the largest global poverty-reduction success in modern history.

After the terrible genocide, President Paul Kagame rebranded Rwanda as the 'Singapore of Africa' and lifted 2 million Rwandans out of poverty.

At forty, after attaining financial independence, I retired from business to devote the rest of my years to social work, founding the Restroom Association of Singapore, World Toilet Organization, BoP Hub, and others along the way.

Following the example of my mother and my country, I believe we can also use entrepreneurship to end poverty for the 4 billion people or half of the population today who still earn below USD 6.85 a day around the world.[5] I started the BoP Hub, another non-profit organization to connect and replicate all poverty solutions to places that need them. Life gives me the opportunity to solve problems for others. I must cherish this chance to be a useful person.

Lesson:

Entrepreneurs don't need a degree to start a business. They use their common sense to convert problems into opportunities.

My Father, Sim Lian How

Lessons from My Father: True Ownership

My father was a provision shop assistant. He earned a very low wage of SGD 90 a month and delivered groceries to the Housing Development Board (HDB) flats. In those days, the lift only served three floors out of ten, and it often broke down. Climbing up ten storeys carrying wooden crates of glass bottle drinks to customers is really hard labour work especially during Chinese New Year when orders for F&N and Green Spot orange drinks are back-to-back.

He was neither educated in Mandarin nor English; he was educated in Teochew dialects back in his childhood in Shantou, China. He always felt sad that as a breadwinner, he was unable to earn enough to feed the family well. He tried to save money by eating dinners at the shop with his boss' family and sleeping on a portable canvas bed along the five-footway outside the shop six nights a week just to save on the 10-cent bus fare for the ride home. Every cent saved was for the family and he told us that he could not even afford 5 cents to drink his favourite soya bean drinks when he was thirsty riding his trishaw to buy provisions, under the hot sun. He simply worked as hard as he could, but as a man of the house, a persistent sense of inadequacy always casted a shadow over my father throughout his life . . . Every time I failed in school, he would be very sad and told me: 'I don't want you to grow up to be like me. Do you want to be like me? Unable to earn enough to feed your family?' He'd beat me whenever I failed, but I knew it hurt in his heart much more than it hurt me.

I didn't understand why I was misbehaving in class and not good in school. I thought I was just born naughty and couldn't help myself. I knew my father loved me, but I was always afraid of him in case he'd beat me for some mistake I'd made inadvertently. I'd always sleep early to avoid him whenever he came home once a week.

Despite my delinquency, my parents loved me and always forgave me. This immense feeling of being loved and protected gave me strength and a sense of security throughout my life. I didn't need to care if others thought I was bad, I knew I was good because my mother loved me. Her love was the most powerful energy that allowed me to continue cheerfully regardless of adversities.

I wished that one day, I could make my parents proud of me. But at that young age, I had no idea how that was ever going to happen.

My relationship with my father got better when I was around fourteen. The income from my mother's businesses brought stability from financial stress and I could see my father becoming more comfortable with himself. In those days, a man was supposed to earn more than his wife, but he had since accepted the fact that having a capable wife is better. As I got to know him, I also absorbed his family values and work ethics. I began to love and appreciate my father. I wanted to be like him—a loving husband, a hard-working and honest man who was responsible towards his family.

The fact that the lift in those days always broke down impacted my father's health and he often collapsed while climbing the stairs.

I told him to stop working at the provision shop when he was nearing seventy. But he told me that his boss was old, and his son was not very good at running the shop. So, he couldn't leave. I told him this is not your shop, and your health is more important.

Then he told me something I'll never forget: 'I've been working here for thirty-five years, if this is not my shop, then whose shop is it?'

That's when I understood that ownership of decisions is more powerful than ownership of shares. When someone trusts you, you want to do your best. I used to think that he merely worked for money, but I suddenly realized that pride can be found even in the most monotonous work. He respected and enjoyed his work and felt a sense of control over the shop.

He fell again during one of the deliveries, and this time, the broken bottles crashed all over him, cutting and bruising him badly. Still, he wanted to get out of the hospital quickly and get back to work. With all the bandages, he told the nurses that he was fine. I knew he would not resign but it was too dangerous for him to continue. I had to find a way to make him leave this job. So, I made a plan with my mother: I applied for a fruit stall license for my mother to sell pineapples at the wet market near our house. I told my father that mum needed his help at the stall, and he had to resign to help his wife. Father loved his wife more than anything in the world. So, he resigned from the provision shop.

After four months, mum told him she was too tired to continue the pineapple stall and they were too old to work so hard any more. After all, the kids were already able to provide enough money for them to relax and enjoy retirement. I thought I did the right thing. We went on many family holidays and now he could see the world.

My father could finally retire and enjoy life. But I was wrong. Without work, he had nothing to look forward to and his health began to deteriorate. He told his wife he was proud that his three kids were all doing well. But for him, he had nothing more to look forward to. He fell ill after some years and soon passed away. Did he die of old age, or due to a lack of self-worth? Or both? I still don't know the answer.

Lesson:

The essayist and dramatist Joseph Addison wrote that there are 'three grand essentials to happiness in this life.' They are 'something to do, something to love, and something to hope for.' When these three things are in good shape, your life and work have meaning.

Learning Deep Human Values

I've had the privilege of having two grandmothers who taught me about traditional Chinese values through storytelling and folktales. They used Chinese proverbs to tell their tales. Each proverb turned into a deep lesson on filial piety, honesty, integrity, patriotism, courage, sacrifice, patience, endurance, righteousness, morals, ethics, humanity, respect, honour, and gallantry.

The memorable ones were about Justice Pao of the Song Dynasty who solved a series of cases in Sherlock Holmes style and brought justice to the common people in each case. I learned patriotism from General Yue Fei who fought bravely for his country despite being betrayed by internal political influence that led to the sacrifice of his life. I learned the importance of honour from the *Romance of Three Kingdoms'* legend of the Taoyuan Brotherhood of Liu Bei, Guan Yu, and Zhang Fei, and how their different strengths and weaknesses complemented each other. There was another Kai Feng Magistrate who was willing to risk the extermination of his entire family in order to press charges against the Empress' sister.

Such lessons were reinforced by regular exposures to Chinese street operas where every story would end with justice prevailing, villains being punished, misunderstandings reconciled, hard work rewarded, and lovers reunited.

Later, I'd watch *Kung Fu* TV series just to listen to the monk sprouting words of wisdom. In school, reading Shakespearean literature, including *Macbeth*, *Merchant of Venice*, *King Lear*, also taught me similar morals. I was never told of any story with an unfair ending. These stories moulded my inner values and character. Because of these experiences, I was unable to accept injustice in society. I was certain that justice must always prevail and everyone has to do whatever it takes to uphold justice. Justice is a public good greater than myself. I am a subordinate and servant to the greater good of the community.

As I grew up, I realized that adults are jaded versions of children. They give up their idealism and innocence. They became afraid and their fear blocks their freedom to learn and experiment as they used to do in their childhood. Children can fight with each other, forgive and reconcile quickly without bearing grudges. They can cry and laugh the next moment, but adults can't because they are too worried about the loss of face and embarrassment. They are even worried about being called childish. I hope I don't have to grow up. I want to remain childlike all my life, no matter how old I become.

Although I knew the ways of the world are complicated, I also knew that if I subdivide any big problems into small slices of questions, and recombine the answers into a main solution, complicated problems can be simplified and understood from a child's view. And everything becomes easier to understand by adults. While the entire society avoids political incorrectness and does not challenge the authorities and the norms, it takes a child to shout that 'The Emperor has no clothes!' so that everyone can suddenly explode into laughter that makes the Emperor realize he is duped. This was how I created the World Toilet Organization to give the Sanitation Agenda its own media centre stage when I saw that it was clearly drowned under the banner of the Water Agenda.

Lesson:

The child in you is pure, simple, idealistic, curious, and imaginative. No matter how you have grown, stay in touch with the child in you and retain your innocence. I hope you will be able to discover your energy from what you love, what inspires you, and what you want to do with your life, by connecting with the beautiful and lovely child inside you, frequently.

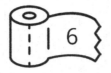

Discovering Who I Am?
What I Discovered from My Comb

Being an under-achiever, I befriended a gangster in my class in Grade 5. Tan Kim Lye told me that he was a member of a secret society and had gone through the rituals of initiations. He educated me on how these illegal secret societies operated according to a set of strict principles to maintain discipline, ethos, honour, and order of brotherhood.

It all sounded like a very fascinating management system, until the day of the Primary School Leaving School Examination (PSLE was an important national milestone examination taken by twelve-year-old students) results announcement. After all the names were called, I was sent to Whitley Secondary School despite my low grades. When I realized that Tan Kim Lye's name had not been called and he was still standing on the other side of the hall together with the other PSLE failures, I remember suddenly thinking to myself: *How sad would my mother feel if my name was not called today?*

I decided that it is better to associate with learned friends thereafter. They seemed more sure of who they were.

In secondary school, my favourite classmate was a nerd and a voracious reader and learner. Koh Poh Chai read years ahead and beyond the school's curriculum. I was deeply influenced by his knowledge in philosophy, history, literature, and human nature. I started to blend the traditional Chinese philosophies taught by my grandmas and parents with the western thinking he taught me.

I also learned that I can have a conversation with myself like a soliloquy inside my head. My imaginary me becomes my best friend.

As a teenager at fourteen, I was trying to discover who I was. I knew that I came from a poor family, was non-athletic, not good-looking, but I wasn't a nerd. Who was I? I wasted lots of time trying to find out what the other kids thought about me and got very diverse opinions that confused me further. Some classmates would tease me as 'girlie', a derogatory term meaning I'm a softie and not masculine enough. Others would call me a 'joker' because I was always telling them jokes I read. Yet, others would praise me for my artistic skills in drawing cartoons and making ceramics pieces. I was also a problem child for the teachers who sent me to stand outside the class, so that I would not be talking in class during the lessons. This branded me as a naughty boy. With bad grades, I was also told that I was stupid. Stupid, girlie, naughty, joker, artist, softie, funny, skinny, failure, crazy, creative, weirdo . . . there were a myriad of labels they tried to stick on me and I had to decide what I wished to be.

In those days, every boy had a comb in their back-pocket and would comb their hair whenever they thought others were looking.

One day, at the canteen, I asked myself: 'Is anyone interested in my hair?' I replied: 'No, I know they're not interested in my hair because I am not interested in their hair. In fact, nobody is interested in anybody's hair except their own.' Upon this realization, I threw away my comb and decided that I would be the only person who could decide who I would be. I loved to read lots of joke books and, sometimes, I found myself laughing unstoppably and loudly inside the library reading these jokes. Since I enjoyed making others laugh with my jokes, I realized that I enjoyed having an audience. The ability to capture a crowd and elicit their responses, gave me a sense of control and knowledge that I could influence people. Using humour to break the ice in communication, I was able to speak frankly and casually to people without being too formal and contrived. I decided it felt good to be a joker, and it became an asset that I could use throughout my life.

I was the Arts Club Chairman of my school, and I loved to draw. I received a lot of feedback that I was creative, I felt admired and important in this area. I decided I will be an artist. Art is about creating ideas, images, visions of something out of virtually nothing, from a blank piece of paper or a lump of clay. The creative process is a form of meditation whereby I can be 'in the zone', a mental state of full immersion, of energized focus, and enjoyment in the process. As art requires lots of experimentation and morphing of ideas, it also led me to become adaptive and entrepreneurial later in life.

It was a very powerful thing for me when I realized that I can actually choose who I define myself to be, without needing any permission from others. It is equally powerful to know who I am not, because it saves me the distractions of trying to become somebody else. I can't be everything to everybody. I can only be who I am best at.

I am an artist and a joker.

With these two niche talents, I felt very comfortable about myself and never had to compete with others on talents that

I didn't have. I put to rest my self-doubts. At parties, if nobody wanted to dance with me, I'd bring out my sketch pad and start sketching pictures to entertain myself. I could live in my own world and not worry about the opinions of others. I found freedom from imposter's syndrome that many teenagers were trapped into. I did not have to try to impress anyone any more. I accepted myself as good enough.

Lesson:

You are the best and only person to decide who you are. You can choose.

My school report card in 1971 at age fourteen

The Out-Standing Student

I was a restless child in class unable to sit still and concentrate on the teachers' lessons.

Instead, I'd be in the back row talking to my classmates and laughing aloud. This irritated the teachers, and I was often sent to stand outside the class so that the teacher could teach without me distracting the class. This was how I became an 'out-standing' student. Standing outside caused me to perform poorly in school. My O-level results were not good enough to allow me to proceed with tertiary education in college or the polytechnic schools.

Having less financial stress by this time, my parents agreed to support my request to attend a private school to take my A-levels as a private student. Our Lady of Lourdes was probably the worst private school in Singapore. We all enrolled in this school because we had failed our O-levels. But the teachers seldom turned up to class, so we played basketball every day and sang in class with guitars. It was like the TV series *Glee*, in real life. We felt guilty wasting our parents' money this way but there was nowhere else where we could go to pursue further education. My classmates were talented in other ways. One of them was a professional shoplifter of luxury goods. Another won a Singapore Talentime TV contest (similar to American Idol today).

When the A-level results came, virtually everyone failed. Except the shoplifter. He was arrested and put in jail for six months before examinations. He had nothing to do in prison, so he studied and got straight A's in all seven subjects. Students like us were not stupid, we simply lacked discipline and the right motivation.

Later on in life, most of my classmates did much better than university graduates. Some became well-known fashion designers, top bond dealers, TV broadcasters, deejays, and one even became the top forex dealer in Singapore. Many started businesses: a classmate who was handicapped with polio started a successful job placement company. It was so successful he was able to buy a bespoke car and fulfilled his dream to drive. Another became a mining tycoon and casino operator in Sri Lanka.

For years I'd been wondering why these school dropouts managed to do so well in society.

After I read about how Finland's educational system emphasizes play, I now know why. At Our Lady of Lourdes, we learned a lot about playing, passion, social skills, humour, and teamwork. As failures, we had nothing to lose. So we looked forward to whatever was possible instead of being limited by the academic route. The school did not plan it that way. They simply gathered all the academic misfits like us who wanted to prove that they were not failures. We all wanted to make our parents proud, and we tried every way to make that happen. The absence of guidance actually allowed us to learn how to organize activities ourselves. In a way, we took control of our curriculum when there were no teachers. Instead of learning from school,

I learned from my classmates that I am not the only misfit in society, that it is OKAY to be who we are, and that it is fun to be who we are. It really feels good this way and it gave me more confidence about myself. We just need to survive while being who we are, and that is what we did. Our Lady of Lourdes was a place that shaped us in many ways, unintentionally.

I eventually enrolled at the Hotel and Catering Training School (HCTS) that provided basic and skilled training for Singaporeans seeking employment in the hotel industry. I learned about how a hotel earns revenue from bedrooms and function rooms. It was the easiest course of study with very low academic content. I graduated and earned my first salary as a room service waiter in the Mandarin Hotel at Orchard Rd. Although the salary was only SGD 90 a month, I learned that being caring, humble, respectful, and joyful can build relationships with customers instantly. As a result, I earned a sizable amount of money through tips. It's hard to describe the feeling of earning your own money. It felt like I was now an independent person. It felt so good to be able to give my mother and father SGD 30 each per month as pocket money, instead of taking money from them. The most delicious meal was at A&W each month, bought with my own earnings.

Though I had a voracious appetite for knowledge as a student, I was naturally averse to formal classroom studies. School, with its test-oriented measures of intelligence, didn't work for me. What worked for me was learning on the job, and meeting new people, where I experienced first-hand the importance of entrepreneurship.

Lesson:

Each of us have unique combinations of multiple talents. Our educational system is only focused on measuring academic excellence and is largely a memory test. Start noticing your talents by doing what you enjoy most. The wider your reading, learning, exposure, and experiences, the higher your ability to combine these skills into useful applications in the future. Conversely, the narrower your knowledge, the fewer your options. Steve Jobs' passion of designing fonts, calligraphy, and typography gave his Macintosh computers a competitive edge with beautiful and intuitive user interface, which created a legacy influencing the design ethos of his legendary company Apple.

My First Job

Like every young Singaporean man, I had to serve two and a half years of national service in the army.

After three months of very tough training, I became a Signaller in the 21st Artillery Battalion. I didn't like physical training under the hot sun, so I proposed to the Regimental Sergeant Major that I could beautify our military camp with mural paintings on the walls. He liked the idea and I became a Camp Artist. I also managed to convince him that I needed two of my room-mates as assistants. The three of us spent one whole year painting all the interior walls in our camp very slowly. The other soldiers were very jealous of us but all the officers liked it. It was a win-win deal.

After my compulsory national military service, my brother, William, told me that there was a vacancy at his workplace, a Swiss company called Diethelm. They needed a site supervisor to oversee a construction project called Peninsula Plaza. Having no experience at all in the construction industry, I told the Division Manager, Mr Chng, that I was keen to learn, and he gave me the job. I worked very hard to fulfil my duties.

I was given a bunch of reflected ceiling building plans, which I could neither read nor understand.

On my first day at the construction site, I introduced myself to my sub-contractor leader, a guy called Yankee-chai who was a former gangster with a body full of tattoos. He replied to me with some expletives, ignored me, and went on working. I realized that I needed to win his friendship in order to be able to supervise him. I bought him coffee and explained that I was new to this trade and had to learn from him. He felt respected thereafter and we became good friends.

However, our entire project was running behind schedule and every trade started blaming the other for the delays. Every weekly site meeting was a quarrelling session with written letters blaming each other. The Project Manager was a guy called SB. Due to my incompetence, he wrote a letter to Mr Chng to have me removed from his jobsite. I thought I was going to be fired, but my boss threw away the letter and told me that he had no time to find another replacement for me. He expected me to resolve the problems between myself and SB.

I was quite happy to be entrusted by my boss to handle the situation. I bought a pack of cigarettes and offered to smoke with SB. He was surprised as he knew I was a non-smoker. I told him that he was right to write that letter as I was really incompetent, but I wanted to learn from him. After a cup of coffee, he became my mentor and taught me how to deflect the blame from other trades. We went on to complete the project successfully. Through this process, I learned that humility and sincerity can work wonders if I am not defensive. Just face the truth and harmonize with others.

My brother alerted me to a new sales vacancy in another department and I applied for it. My job was to sell movable ballroom partitions for hotels. Suddenly, the knowledge from my course on hotel banqueting operations became useful. I was given the job and went on to become the top salesman in that department earning very good commissions of SGD 4,000 per month on average. That was a lot of money for a school failure.

I was very happy as a salesman until Mr Chng left and was replaced by a nasty new boss, Mr Ang, a micromanager who belittled the performance of all his staff without offering any new ideas. His superiority complex was so toxic that everyone wanted to leave the company. There were eighty resignations that year in our division. Although only about half of us actually left, the new recruits left faster than us, and even their replacements left too. This was how hostile the environment became with the arrival of the new Division Manager. Meanwhile, I was invited to become the Singapore Mercantile and Manual Workers Union Secretary of Diethelm Branch. The Branch Union Chairman and Vice Chairman told me very frankly that they each had two years more before their pension was due and could not afford to take any strong union action in order to have smooth exits with loyalty bonuses. They had both worked for Diethelm for thirty-five years as clerks and would retire at fifty-five from their posts as senior clerks.

I accepted this volunteer role because this was my chance to learn management skills from the other side of the negotiation table. I had 2,200 union members under my care. However, since there were so many complaints against my Division Manager, Mr Ang, I was unable to maintain a good working relationship with him. One day, Ang called me into his office and gave me two choices: I could either go out there and persuade everyone that he was a good boss 'with a good gospel', or he'd employ a second salesman to share my commission. He said: 'Please take this as an advice and not a threat.' I immediately reported his threat to Union HQ and a letter was written to our Swiss

Managing Director. Our relationship had become untenable and I knew I had to leave soon.

My brother, William, resigned with his Department Manager, Kenny Quek, to set up their own business called BES. I started thinking if I should look for a new job, or if I should start a new business like William and Kenny did. That's when a sales colleague Nicholas Koh told me that he has found an investor, Mr T, who can invest SGD 100,000 for both of us to start a new company giving us 20 per cent shares each upon us attaining a profit of SGD 100,000. We set up our first company in early 1983 and started our first business venture trading with imported building materials, selling them to new construction projects in Singapore and Southeast Asia.

Six months after we left Diethelm, Ang was fired, and I remember thinking I should have stayed if I had known that he was going to be fired. But it was too late. I had already started my first company.

Lesson:

Humility and respect can build great relationships. Arrogance and disrespect will alienate people.

The Power of Hate

Starting a brand-new company in 1983, I wanted to become the exclusive distributor for famous European brands of high quality building materials, import them and sell them to Singapore and Southeast Asia. The year 1983 was the official birthday of the internet but it had not yet reached Singapore. We were still using the telex system that transmitted and received written messages using teletypewriters and perforated paper tapes. It was cheaper to write paper letters and send them via airmail, although the mail took a long time to reach and was sometimes lost in transit.

I went to the Trade Libraries of the German embassy, UK Trade Commission, French embassy, and United States Information Service Libraries. I shortlisted the potential suppliers and wrote 100 snail mails offering to be their distributor for Singapore. Once they showed interest, we communicated through telex, which was more costly. The facsimile machine only arrived a few years later. We seldom used overseas phone calls as IDD charges were based on six-second blocks and very expensive as well.

Within three months, I managed to secure the exclusive distributorship of a new brand of movable walls from Germany called Huppe and a new brand of French roofing tiles called TBF, and business was good. The market was buying Malaysian concrete roofing tiles at 80 cents per tile, but I was selling the French clay roof tiles at SGD 2.50 per tile. When the first developer who liked the product asked me why he should pay three times for my roofing tiles, I told him he was only paying a 2 per cent increase in the overall construction cost of the houses but he could sell his houses faster and at higher prices if he designed the entire architecture into a Spanish villa complete with arches and stucco walls. I did not just sell the product, I sold him an entire value proposition and business opportunity. He liked my proposal and sold his houses very quickly. Since his project was along a very busy road, the natural orange clay roofs enjoyed high street-visibility and suddenly, customers started trying to find out its supplier and looking for us. I began to understand that the 'pull' strategy works faster than 'push' or hard-selling.

By 1984, our company made a good profit of about SGD 150,000 in that eighteen-month partnership period and we were given 20 per cent share certificates each. However, within eighteen months, our investor, Mr T fell in love with his secretary, and wanted to divorce his wife. Things started to get complicated. His company was owned by his wealthy wife, whom we had never met. This meant that our partnership would be with his wife if he had a divorce. To secure his future income, he started a second company with his secretary and her brother to sell roofing tiles from another French factory, next door to our supplier's factory in France.

We never met his wife, and we decided that a partnership with T was unsustainable. Nicholas and I left to set up a new business with Kenny Quek and William Sim, becoming rivals with T in the roof tiles business. The new company was called Besco. Our suppliers, TBF and Huppe, followed us.

Nicholas and I hated T, and he hated us, too, as competitors. Over a period of three years, we competed so hard in the marketplace that amazingly instead of destroying each other, we killed all the other roof tiles competitors and took 50 per cent of the roof tiles market share each in Singapore. Our promotion was so vigorous that the entire market transformed into a fully clay roofing tile business and not a single piece of concrete tile was sold thereafter.

I was happy with our new success but felt that hatred was not good for the soul. I asked a mutual friend to arrange lunch with T. It was a strange meeting between T, Nicholas, and me. It was all smiles when I thanked him for the good fight that brought both of us success. He laughed in agreement. We didn't talk a lot, but a healing process happened during that lunch. We did not need forgiveness. There was no need to speak about right or wrong. We simply accepted the current reality. At the end of the lunch, we shook hands, mouthed some niceties, and I felt a big heavy rock roll off my heart. I was now free from the burden of hatred, and it was a great relief.

Lessons:

1. You give more value when you sell solutions instead of selling products.
2. While hatred can be self-destructive, emotions are neither good nor bad, they are useful. The important lesson here was to not let hate consume me, but instead to channel it constructively.
3. Learn to 'let go' and move on. Don't carry past emotional baggage if you want to live a happy life. It doesn't matter

who is right. What matters is how to be free from unnecessary emotional distractions.

4. Follow your feelings and find the most balanced answer.

Starting Again

Logo of Besco Building Supplies SEA Pte Ltd, the
company I set up in 1984

After splitting up with Mr T in 1984, Kenny Quek and my
brother, who owned BES company, invested SGD 100,000 for
Nicholas and I to start a new company called Besco Building
Supplies. Nicholas and I would own 20 per cent of free shares
each once we made SGD 100,000 net profits. We both drew
a salary of SGD 2,200 and were so frugal, we did not rent
an office. Nicholas and I would work from the coffee shop
downstairs of our parent company BES in Bukit Merah and
wait till their sales and site staff left the office every morning

before we occupied their seats to work. It was nice to have air-conditioning instead of the fans at the coffee shop.

Both Nicholas and I did not understand cash flow planning. We collected payments as we sold our products. And when our cash was low, our banker would call us to tell us that our cheque had bounced, and we would need to quickly top up the cash. We'd switch focus to chase payments and pay up. Sometimes, we pleaded with our suppliers to give us more time to repay them. It was a crazy way of doing business but it was also the only way we knew at that time. We did not even know how much money we had made until next year when our auditor told us the results. All we knew were our rough numbers by using a rule of thumb, which gave us a broadly accurate estimate. Because of good relationships built over time, the banks and suppliers were very accommodating.

A year later, we managed to rent the office next door for SGD 800 a month and employed six staff. We worked from 10 a.m. to 10 p.m. daily. I remember feeling restless on weekends and grumbling why Singapore should have so many public holidays while I worked through all these holidays and weekends.

Like my hardworking parents, I was a workaholic, and I also expected my staff to work long hours like me. For the first two years, they enjoyed the spirit of camaraderie as we worked like a strong team. We started at 10 a.m. and ended the day at 10 p.m. Furthermore, I'd buy them supper and we'd chat for an hour or more while we ate. However, as they started to find spouses, they were quite unhappy and saw me as a slave driver instead. In the third year, five of them resigned together en bloc. At that time, I could not understand why they had lost their drive? So, I simply employed another six new staff and worked them hard again, with long hours from 10 a.m. to 10 p.m. I was focused on beating the competition and building a strong company.

Our diligence gave us the advantage of the speed of service. As every project was different, our clients received their proposals complete with drawings, plans, and quotations the next day and this gave us an edge over competitors who always took longer. Our sales and profits doubled over the next year. But after two more good years, I faced yet another en bloc resignation, where five staff who felt the effects of overwork left. Again, I employed another six new staff, and our business grew again. I was an unrepentant slave driver. I was oblivious to their feelings because I felt that there was no room for laziness. I'd learn later that I was wrong, when I started dating seriously and had to go home to my future wife. I stopped being a slave driver after that.

Looking back, I have to thank my nasty boss, Mr Ang, because he was the one who motivated me to leave my good job to start my own business. If my original boss, Mr Chng, had not left, I might have stayed on and been a salaried man all my life. While Mr Ang probably didn't know his flaws, I too did not know mine. Many of my staff left to start their own businesses and they are likely to have said the same about me. I lacked such empathy in those days; I was simply oblivious of their feelings.

Lesson:

It is easy to criticize others, but not easy to criticize oneself. Our flaws may be noticed by others but not by ourselves.

Suddenly Married

Throughout my adolescent years, my grandmother indoctrinated in me the belief that a man needs to be capable to win respect from his wife. She taught me that there is no point being a romantic but poor guy, who would surely be despised later by his wife for not being able to provide for the family. So, I worked hard to ensure I could provide my future wife and family with the security of a financially strong husband.

I had a series of four girlfriends, but they all left me in a row because I was a workaholic and never really spent quality time with them. My priority then was always work and business. But something happened on my thirtieth birthday. Suddenly, I felt that I wasn't a young man any more and decided that I had to get married before I became too old. I began to seriously look out for a spouse. I started dating Joanne, a girl ten years younger than me. That was when I needed to leave the office at 7 p.m. to go have dinner with my girlfriend, and suddenly I realized that the other staff should be allowed to do the same. I stopped expecting them to work till 10 p.m. I left it up to them to decide what time they needed to leave, as I would leave at 7 p.m. every evening.

After a whirlwind romance with Joanne, we got married within twelve months. My family advised me not to marry such a young girl, she was, after all, only twenty-one years old. They said she didn't look ready for marriage. I defied everyone and made my own decision.

But problems started to brew. She was disappointed that after marriage I wanted her to stay at home each night and go out only on weekends. She'd go out by herself and come back reeking of alcohol. One morning, my staff told me he saw my wife at a bar drinking by herself and there were guys touching her as she looked tipsy.

I reflected and realized that we both married for the wrong reasons. I married her because I felt old at thirty-one. She married me because her parents were always fighting, and she wanted a refuge to escape from the daily family disputes. I asked her if she thought we should continue our marriage. She said she needed her freedom back. We went to the lawyer to end the marriage. In Singapore, it takes three years before a divorce can be finalized, even with mutual agreement. It was fortunate that we didn't have children. We parted amicably.

Six months before the legal termination of my first marriage, I was visiting Mr Teng, my distributor in Kuala Lumpur, Malaysia. I told him that I once asked my father why he didn't buy any land when land was so cheap, but he replied that he never had spare cash. In order not to miss the boat, I thought of land banking for the long term. He told me that if I wanted to buy land near Singapore, I should contact his sister, Julie, who worked as a secretary at a law office in Johor Bahru across the causeway in Malaysia. He called her and I spoke to her to make an appointment. After I put the phone down, I teased Teng that Julie's voice is so sweet, I might want to be his brother-in-law. He thought I was joking.

I met Julie in a coffee house near her office. I remember her wearing a red dress with her hair falling over one eye. She was so beautiful. I was mesmerized that day and I invited her for dinner and a movie in Singapore. She accepted.

We only dated for six months, but this time, I did not marry rashly. I got my brother, William, to give me his opinion. He told me she'll make a good wife, and that is so true. I was so lucky to have found her. She moved to Singapore once we got married. Finding love is the biggest prize of life. We've been married for thirty-three years now, and I'm still crazily in love with her. (We still have the ten-acre plot of land in Johor Bahru that I hope to build into a Singapore nostalgia 1960s village one day.)

Looking back, nothing was planned. Things just happened as opportunities arrived.

I do not believe that if you fail to plan, you plan to fail. To me, it just sounds good only because it rhymes.

I believe that you can plan but luck plays a major role in success. One way you can increase your luck is to keep a good reputation with other people so that they'll refer their friends to you. There is an Asian traditional belief called karma, which is the belief of the chain relationship between cause and effect. It cannot be scientifically proven but I read somewhere that karma is basically asynchronized reciprocity. In a synchronous transaction, what you give and what you get are pre-agreed. In asynchronous reciprocity, I may do someone a favour and expect no reward. But that person who received my help might tell other people about his experience with me and this increased my reputation without me knowing.

If I keep doing good as a natural habit and not as an exchange of favours, the waves of reciprocity propagate continuously, like a pay-it-forward formula. The person I've helped might also go on to help someone else and if the momentum grows, that society we live in also becomes culturally more liveable and pleasant.

Lesson:

If a relationship is unsustainable, don't prolong the suffering. Solve all problems as amicably as possible. As one chapter closes, another may open for the better.

What to Do with a Big Mistake

I became the distributor of a top-quality ballroom movable partition product and was able to use my knowledge of hotel operations to help hotel operators design the best flexible layout configurations to maximize their profits. I also read up deeply on acoustics knowledge to increase my ability to provide a high degree of soundproofing between rooms. Our brand of partitions, Huppe, soon became highly desirable in the market.

In my second year of Besco, I won the bid to supply Movable Walls for a big project called Raffles City Convention Centre. Nicholas and I treated ourselves for the first time to an expensive dinner at Oberoi Hotel's Rang Mahal restaurant. We wanted to experience success. So, we ordered champagne and cigars. The North Indian food was delicious, but we choked on the cigars and did not actually like the taste of alcohol.

I was rejoicing with my team when I received a call from Tan Hang Lee, my former colleague at Diethelm who was now my competitor. He informed me that I'd made an error and grossly underpriced my bid. He even told me the page of the tender document where the mistake was. I checked it thoroughly and realized that he was right! Suddenly, I was overcome with gloom. I've underpriced my bid by SGD 1.1 million! My bid was SGD 1.81 million, his bid was SGD 3.3 million and the third bid was SGD 4.4 million. He told me to give up my bid so that he could win.

I could not sleep for the next few days. I did not know what I was supposed to do. I was so young, and I feared that I'd become bankrupt soon. At the awards meeting, I went to Raffles City and told them honestly that I'd made a mistake in my bid and could not accept their award. They warned me that they could sue me as the bid was legally binding. I told them I was ready to be sued since the damages I'd need to pay them would be less than the SGD 1.1 million losses if I accepted the bid. After some deliberation among themselves, they asked me if I'd accept the contract if they raised the price to SGD 2.92 million so that I'd not suffer any losses. I was pleasantly surprised with their offer and accepted it. Their additional condition was that my German supplier had to jointly sign the contract. I immediately called Germany and they agreed to this term. We thought we were all happy again but there were more obstacles ahead.

My happiness was short-lived. I realized due to the small size of our company and low paid-up capital of SGD 100,000, no bank would give me the credit facility to finance this million-dollar project. I needed to open a letter of credit to buy the goods from Germany and also to bridge our cash flow for the period between goods delivery and payment by Raffles City. I'd bitten off more than I could chew. After getting rejected by four banks, I was feeling desperate when DBS Bank suddenly called me to offer their banking facilities. They told me they did not need collateral securities because Raffles City was owned by them.

I was so lucky to have survived my inexperience in that early stage of life as an entrepreneur. There was so much that I didn't know, but each time, luck came along to help me. If I were religious, I'd certainly say there was a guardian angel guiding me.

Lessons:

When confused, just tell the truth and face the music. Admitting a mistake is not as difficult as it seems. Your competitor might actually be your saviour. If Tan had not alerted me of my mistake, I might have ignorantly signed the contract and gotten into a very big trouble.

Luck plays a big role in success, although most successful people won't admit it.

How to Become Cleverer than You Are

Because I am always dreaming of doing things that I am not familiar with, I am often clueless on how to get things done. Here are a few tactics and coping mechanisms I've devised to manage my brain.

Tactic 1: Self-Dialogue

Whenever I don't know how to solve a problem, I split myself into two Jacks like two intimate friends having an honest dialogue with each other. I can have a dialogue with myself anytime, instantly. Many people talk to themselves, too, but the stories we tell ourselves must not be defensive nor negative. Defensive self-talk can limit my vision. Negative self-talk can lead to depression. I have to practise honest self-dialogue as two panellists in a debate. Since this is a perfectly private conversation, there is no risk of embarrassment or insults. The dialogue needs to be pragmatic and constructive to seek solutions, acceptance, and peace of mind.

Here's an example:

Once I told a friend her weaknesses when she was unprepared to hear them. I could see she was visibly upset when she left. I felt I shouldn't have been so curt. So, I dialogue with myself:

Jack 1: What happens now?
Jack 2: I don't know. I was stupid to do that.
Jack 1: Do you want to apologize?
Jack 2: Do you think that'll help?
Jack 1: I don't know either. It might make things worse.
Jack 2: How will you feel the next time you meet her?
Jack 1: Awkward.
Jack 2: Can you pretend nothing happened and be as cheerful as before with her?
Jack 1: I can do that. This might be better.
Jack 2: How do you think she'll react?
Jack 1: I can only know after I try.

I met her again and did not mention the incident. We were both cordial with each other, but I sensed that she wanted to put things behind us, so I apologized. She told me she thought over what I had said and felt that only a true friend would tell her that. She appreciated my candour, but it took time for her to recover from the initial shock. We became even closer friends after that incident.

Tactic 2: Invoke a Wiser Person

Jack 1: What would a wiser person do if he was confronted with this problem?
Jack 2: He'd probably do this . . .

And I'd solve the problem by supplying the answers to myself by leveraging the imaginary wiser person inside my own mind. I've often invoked Lee Kuan Yew when I was younger, now I invoke whoever is best suited. As in the Raffles City example that was mentioned earlier, I was totally stressed about the mistake I made in underpricing the tender price. I was clueless as to what I should do. So I asked myself if Lee Kuan Yew was faced with this problem, what would he do? Using his moral values and ethos, I decided that facing the truth is the best solution. That was how I ended up winning the contract despite my error of underpricing it by SGD 1.1 million.

As you can see, imagining that I was in the shoes of Lee Kuan Yew allowed me to become wiser than I originally was. This method allows me to summon all kinds of experts in each subject without even engaging them.

Tactic 3: Simplify

When a problem is complicated and/or complex, I divide such a problem into small slices of expert areas. Then, I start to solve the easier slices or low-hanging fruits. I may also seek expert advice in each of these areas. This can be done by reading the experts' publications, talking to some of them, or forming a group chat. Another way is to look for course brochures of that particular subject and read the headings on the content page of the course curriculum. These headings usually give me insights into how to frame a solution pattern, although I need to use them selectively and adaptively. I string these answers into discussions between all the experts and develop the most plausible options and go into more granular details after narrowing the scope of possibilities. This allows me to start orchestrating the right tool for the right job. In this way, I become an expert in doing what I can't do, by mobilizing others who can.

Tactic 4: Meeting of Emotions

I've not yet fully mastered this method, but I've tried it often. When I am confused by emotions, I summon all my relevant emotions and sit them in the 'boardroom' of my mind. These emotions could include anger, courage, envy, anxiety, disgust, embarrassment, frustration, shame, guilt, boredom, disappointment, satisfaction, surprise, pride, sadness, and others.

I would ask each of my emotions for answers as to why I felt in certain ways, and how I should handle them or behave going forward. When I seek their help, I accept their presence with a degree of respect. And they respond to me with similar respect. Sometimes, I forgive them, and they also forgive me. Acknowledging one's emotions is an important step in self-awareness. This is a tactic that I still need lots of practice with because it requires calmness to deal with such a wide range of characters inside my head. Initially, I grouped them broadly under fear and love, but as I went on my inner discovery journey, I learned that each emotion is unique and cannot be stereotyped and I need to accept them as legit so that I can seek their advice for the best way forward in each new situation.

Tactic 5: Sanctuary

In my younger days, when everything was beyond my control, I created a 'sanctuary' inside my mind where I could escape from the noises and be safe. This 'sanctuary' is a cave where I can hide from everyone. Suddenly, there is nobody around any more to disturb or distract me and it allows me time to find clarity and calmness. It is my favourite hiding place from chaotic situations. Physically, I could be in my room or sitting in a garden or a bench in the park or a field. Mentally, I am alone inside a safe place. I never knew how to meditate but this was a much faster way to avoid stress. I once saw a *Peanuts* comic strip where Linus van Pelt is saying, 'No problem is so big or so complicated that it can't be run away from!' I pick up pragmatic philosophies from the most unlikely places. I design all kinds of coping mechanisms at different ages. Nowadays, I seldom use this method because I have become less afraid of life.

Tactic 6: Detachment

Detachment is the abandonment of cravings. Our pains are largely caused by our cravings. If we minimize our cravings, we minimize our pains. When aspirations become painful, I moderate them, and wait to try another time. Don't force an unnatural outcome. Let the universe decide. If it was meant to be, it'll come back. If it was not meant to be, it'll not. A person is at his freest when he does not crave more than he already has. Appreciation as a basis of happiness is a virtue of Buddhist teaching. I draw lessons from all sources including religions, sages, and thinkers.

Lessons:

You are your own best friend and you should maintain this relationship by being completely honest and frank with yourself. In this way, you can avoid self-denial and attitudes of defensiveness. If you can manage yourself, it is much easier to manage the outside world.

Everything is a state of mind. We see things according to the stories we tell ourselves, which interpret each situation accordingly. Master the art of telling yourself the stories that can help you find the answers you need.

How I Became a Serial Businessman:
Maybricks, 1987

Immerse yourself totally into the business and think about it in your waking hours as well as in your dreams. When you become the spirit of your mission, there is nothing to lose and there is nothing to fear.

I was the Arts Club Chairman during my secondary school days. I learned about the nature of clay—porcelain, stoneware, earthenware, and terracotta. I learned how each type of clay behaves, how to handle it, how to shape it, dry it, glaze it, and fire it into beautiful ceramic pieces.

It was all for fun, but later in life, this knowledge allowed me to set up the biggest clay bricks factory and the biggest clay roof tile factory in Malaysia.

During the mid-1980s, Singapore was in a construction boom. I saw so many construction sites popping up. There was a shortage of bricks and prices were rising.

I found a physicist who was an expert in modern bricks, who could manage the entire design and building process. We found a traditional bricks factory in Johor with 100 acres of quarry land to become our partners. We made a simple one-page plan and saw that the numbers were very profitable. Since we were surrounded by sawmills, we could substitute petroleum fuel, required for firing the bricks, with sawdust. This gave us a competitive edge with tremendous energy cost savings.

Besco injected 20 per cent cash as shares. We valued the quarry land as 40 per cent shares for the landowners, and the physicist got 40 per cent shares for his technical planning and project management fees. We borrowed 80 per cent of the start-up capital from the bank, completed construction of an automatic tunnel dryer and tunnel kiln, and started production. The quality of the bricks produced was good and our energy saving technology succeeded. We branded it Maybricks.

Market prices of bricks were much higher than originally anticipated, but the physicist partner got greedy. He offered to buy all our shares paying 1.50 ringgit for every 1 ringgit. He said that since he was the only one who knew how to operate the factory, we had no choice but to sell our shares to him. Otherwise, he could sell his shares to us on the same terms, but we'd not know how to operate the factory. This was a bullying tactic. I persuaded the landowner not to sell but to buy the physicist's shares. However, we didn't have the money, so we had to find someone else to buy the shares.

Miraculously, the landowner found a buyer from a religious temple of which he was a member. We were shocked that the religious leader wrote him a cheque without even looking at the books or visiting the factory. When asked why he trusted us immediately, the religious leader replied that this partnership was arranged by destiny. Seven days after we paid the physicist to buy out his shares, he left and the factory suddenly stopped operating. We were in a quandary when the owner of Tajo Bricks next door came over. He heard that we were bullied by the physicist and decided to teach us how to operate our factory. We were surprised that a competitor would help us in our most dire hour. He told us that he used to be an unhappy partner of that physicist and he didn't want to see others bullied by him. The shutdown was caused by a seven-day shutdown timer switch programmed by the disenchanted physicist. He simply turned it on again, and the factory started roaring production once more. He helped us recruit some experienced workers and Maybricks went on to be very profitable over the next two decades.

I could not understand how these serendipities occurred in such a timely manner, saving the day each time we were in trouble. Perhaps the religious leader was right about destiny, but I remain clueless till today.

Lesson:

Be calm and assertive in the face of a bully. Tell others your plight and enlist help.

The Peranakan-8 roof tile I designed for the
conservation of heritage houses

TBF (Terreal) 1989

Mr Jean-Luc Muary-Laribiere was the son of the owner of our French roofing tiles supplier, and I loved doing business with him. We would visit his factory in a small village called Roumazières-Loubert once or twice a year, and he'd bring us to eat at châteaus (castles) in the Charente region between Bordeaux and Cognac or entertain us in Paris.

He made a bet with his father that he could sell 100 x 40 feet containers of roofing tiles per year to Singapore, and if he did so profitably, his father would retire and let him take over as CEO. His father loved the idea but doubted that there were many roofs in Singapore that needed so much tile, since the roofs of our public housing flats and condominiums had flat roofs and not pitched roofs. We decided to help Jean-Luc win the bet and went on promoting tiles to linkways from bus stops to public housing as shelters from rain. These linkways became a norm and added to the volumes needed for schools, mosques, and landed housing. We also jointly designed about fifty-five accessory tiles that were not available with our competitors and this gave us large profit margins as well. I even designed one tile called the Peranakan-8 tile that fused eight pieces of traditional Straits Settlements old tiles into a modern tile with proper drainage. Jean-Luc won the bet and became CEO of TBF.

In 1989, our roofing tile business was booming in Singapore. But at the same time, TBF was also enjoying a boom time in France. Unfortunately, too much of a good thing isn't always the best. Both businesses were doing so well that our French factory could not fulfil our orders in time. The deliveries were late, customers were starting to get nervous, and Besco was in big trouble as we forecasted further delays.

I was in a conundrum that I had never experienced before, but I could lose their trust. In order to ensure that customers got their delivery on time, I had no choice but to buy products from all my competitors to fulfil the orders. The competitors were all laughing as they sold this to me at high prices without any discount.

That year, I lost SGD 1.5 million in order to keep our promised delivery dates.

The competitors spread the news that my company was unreliable in delivery and customers should switch to them. They also told everyone that I had to buy materials from them and was suffering deep losses. After the crisis, to our surprise, our reputation actually shot up as the customers trusted us even more. My customers and the entire market heard about how I was willing to suffer losses so as to keep our promises and honour our delivery dates. Our business grew better than before as our good reputation benefited from the heavy promotion by our competitors.

I also did not claim compensation from our French manufacturer, as I treasured our long-term relationship, something that they appreciated very much. Our imported roofing tiles business was growing at such a rapid pace, we started to sell to Malaysia and other regional markets.

Lesson:

Relationships are more valuable than money. Reputation and trust must be preserved at all costs. Money can be earned back as long as reputation and friendships are robust.

Problems Can Be Solved

Due to the high inheritance taxes in France, Jean-Luc's father decided to sell their TBF shares to Saint Gobain, the largest glass company in the world. Meanwhile, Saint Gobain decided that we should produce in Malaysia instead of paying shipping cost, which was 50 per cent of the cost of the tiles. TBF bought 50 per cent of Besco's shares and we used the money from the shares sold to invest in a Malaysian TBF factory with 100 million ringgit as capital.

We submitted a proposal to the Malaysia Industrial Development Authority and were told to meet a top government official in Johor state where we intended to locate the factory. In our meeting, the top government official told us that our project is too large, and we may face lots of delays in the approval process. He told us that if we gave 20 per cent free shares to his friend, he'd help us get all the approvals efficiently. He emphasized that having the 'right partner' was the key to success in Malaysia and if we became his partner, we could have a good future. As we left the meeting, my French partner told me to abort our investment plans since we could not be involved in bribery.

I didn't know the solution. So, I tricked my brain to find an answer. I asked myself: 'What would our Prime Minister Lee Kuan Yew do if he was confronted with this challenge?' Our Prime Minister is known for his incorruptible character and when I invoked his avatar, I found the answer. This imaginary game that I sometimes play is rather useful, to make myself cleverer than I am.

I approached the Chairman of the Johor State Economic Development Corporation and offered to sell him 20 per cent shares at par value for cash. He liked our proposal and appointed a subsidiary company, Johor Land, to invest in our factory. Johor Land was a large housing developer in Johor, and they became both an investor and a regular customer of our roofing tiles. We did not have to pay any bribes and got all our approvals efficiently. Our factory opened successfully in 1994 in Kluang.

In order to build the clay roof tiles factory, I needed to first be able to discover a huge deposit of terracotta clay quarries. The clay had to meet very specific qualities of colour, plasticity, porosity, shrinkage tolerances, and stability in supply at very low prices. I was clueless where to find such clay deposits. It also needed to be near the new factory located near a gas pipeline so that the colour of the fired roof tiles would be more consistent as compared to when using any other fuel. At first, I asked real estate agents to look for low-cost quarry land near a gas pipeline so that we do not incur high cost of transportation of clay to the factory. I tried many times, digging 20 kilograms of clay samples and sending them to France for testing, but all the samples failed to pass the stringent criteria. I was clueless when one day I saw a truckload of beautiful clay bricks with the colours I was looking for. I asked the driver and discovered the factory was in Yong Peng, about 40 kilometres from the factory in Kluang Industrial Park that sits on a gas pipeline.

I drove to Yong Peng and found the right clay quarries. However, these lands were Malay reserve lands that could not be sold to non-Malays. Instead of buying the land, I signed with the land owners a long-term contract to buy their clay at a fixed price and secured a stable supply of the raw material for our clay roof tile factory.

Lesson:

Even when you are clueless, you must continue to believe there is an answer waiting to meet you. It is like believing there is a girl waiting to marry you. Because of this belief, you will continue looking and find the answers. Do not ask the question 'Can I?' because this question may lead to self-doubt. Ask the question 'How can I?' because this question helps you focus on finding the way forward to achieve success.

Nest Development

In 1986, Nicholas Koh suggested that we venture into another unknown area, property development, and become real estate developers. At that time, the big developers like City Development and Far East Organization were not interested in small developments. So, we could still buy small land parcels at reasonable prices. Kenny, William, and I liked the idea. We roped in a few other friends and started Nest Development.

Although we were novices, we learned very quickly that this required very little internal resources. We borrowed 90 per cent of the money from the banks to buy the land and pay for the construction cost. We used the bank's money to pay the architect to design the building and the contractor to build it. We paid real estate agents a commission when they sold our units on plan before construction. We paid the bank with the sales proceeds and kept a nice profit of about 15 per cent for ourselves. The real return on cash investments could have been as much as 50 per cent within two years. Our first project was a row of fourteen houses at Rosyth Terrace. It sold very fast, and we proceeded to buy other plots and sell the houses on plans.

The cash flow was very good since the property market was growing all the time.

I started to understand more about how to use other people's money, other people's talents, and other people's aspirations. I began to develop the Leverage Model for everything else to grow them faster.

One morning, I came back to the office and told my brother, Kenny, and Nicholas that I'd bought sixteen heritage shophouses. They knew I didn't have money to buy sixteen properties. I told them I only had money for the 1 per cent deposit and I'd paid the deposit. I could not resist because it was so cheap, I was certain that they'd like to take some. It was cheap because the sixteen units were in one title deed and it was not easy to find a buyer urgently. We found four other friends to team up, applied for subdivision into sixteen individual house titles, and I've kept my two units until today, collecting rental income for my future retirement. By breaking bulk and sharing the benefits, I managed to buy for myself the two units at a very low total price of SGD 250,000. Today, these shophouses are worth SGD 11 million and still rising.

Lessons:

When you work in cohesive teams, you give each other courage to embark on new ideas and share risk.

The Leverage Model allows you to use very little internal resources and very large external resources.

Catch the economic growth trends, and ride on it.

Australian International
School Investments

If you find an unmet need, you've found a gold mine. All you have to do is to act on it.

One morning in 1992, our major shareholder, Kenny Quek, told me that last night at the Cricket Club, some Australian guy was complaining that there was no Australian International School in Singapore, and someone ought to start one. The Aussie kids were going to the American School, the United World College and the Tanglin Trust, instead, and when they went home to Australia, they had to fit the Australian curriculum, which could be inconvenient and disruptive.

I told him that that was a golden opportunity. But we didn't know how to do it.

So, we appointed an Australian consultant to draw out the plans. He recruited Miss Coral Dixon of the famous Ravenswood School for Girls from Sydney, and he brought eight Australian partners to invest 50 per cent of the shares, while on our side we had eight Singaporeans investing in the other 50 per cent shares. All sixteen shareholders had no background in education.

We simply trusted our principal to run the show since she had all the experience.

Sixteen of us invested a total of SGD 1 million, which in those days was small enough that we could afford to lose it. In 1993, we started with 32 students on day one, in a rented space owned by the Methodist Church on Sophia Road. We lost money for the first three years. Then it grew to 250 students, such that we had to move to Emerald Hill, to the space vacated by the Singapore Chinese Girls School. Thereafter, we started making money.

Soon, enrolment grew larger, and we had to move to the Ulu Pandan space vacated by the American School. When we hit 800 students, we had nowhere to go and had to build our own school. Schools are a fixed cost business. After our revenue exceeded the fixed cost, the rest of the increase in student numbers were virtually pure profits. Each year, we were able to issue dividends between SGD 1 and 3 million.

But when we went to Singapore Land Authority (SLA), we were told that the American School, United World College, and a whole list of others were in the queue for building land. So, we would not be able to get land for at least the next ten years.

We were frustrated when we read in the newspaper that Singtel, the largest local Singapore telecommunications company, wanted to buy Optus Telco in Australia. We immediately met the Australian High Commissioner to request for a clause to be added in the negotiations. Namely, to request for land to expand the Australian International School so as to accommodate the Australian community here. Our request was granted, and we were offered a choice of three parcels of land by SLA.

We chose the plot on Lor Chuan that had high street visibility along the Central Expressway and went on to build a brand new school. Because the business model was very cash positive, we were able to borrow the entire construction and land cost from the bank, 100 per cent without personal guarantees being required! Our school grew to 3,500 students from fifty countries.

In our eighteenth year, we sold our school to Cognita Schools for SGD 105 million and most of the sixteen shareholders went into retirement. Coral Dixon also retired. We were glad that we created an international school that was ranked third, after the American School and United World College, at that time. Cognita Schools went on to expand the school with the land next to it and made even more money than we ever could do ourselves.

Lessons:

Mingle with frustrated people. Unhappy people who complain are potential sources of opportunities, as they help you identify problems. Convert them into business opportunities and models.

You don't need to know how to do it, you can invest in professionals to do it. If you have an idea, begin. Once you begin, the way will find you, while you find the way. If you don't begin, you will never know.

Crisis Management: How to Mentally Cope with a Recession

Since I became an entrepreneur, I was rather lucky to ride the wave of an upward economic cycle in Singapore and Malaysia, but like they say, what goes up must come down.

In October 1997, the Asian Currency Crisis hit Singapore. Businesses started to deteriorate. As each month passed, business became worse. New orders were dwindling, prices were down, and the competition was fierce.

In the beginning, I heard that people were losing jobs. Then my friends were losing their jobs. Then I heard of companies going bankrupt. Then my friends' companies went bankrupt. The entire society was surrounded by gloom and pessimism.

In 2000, at the deepest part of the recession in Singapore, our businesses were facing grave difficulties. We cut losses in our real estate businesses, sold the remaining properties at a loss and closed them down. Our factories were overstocked, and we had to cut employee headcount and reduce production capacities.

Then the shock. Our French partner, Saint Gobain, wanted to pull out of Asia and sell us their 50 per cent shares. If we did not agree, they wanted Besco to close down. That was followed by a second shock. After sixteen years of friendship, my local business partners, Kenny and Nicholas, also wanted to sell their shares on the same terms as the French. This was the first business we founded but market pessimism had shaken everyone. They all wanted out.

It was really stressful. I didn't want to close the company down. After the French partners bought 50 per cent of Besco, I was only a 10 per cent shareholder and my brother, William, only held 5 per cent shares, but we were emotionally attached to Besco. And this emotional attachment became a painful thing. I felt powerless looking at my forty staff and thinking of their families. I had been working with them like a family. Many of them had been working with me for more than ten years. We were a happy bunch and now the macro-economic cycle had hit us unprepared.

My French partners offered to sell the shares at book value, which was quite low after they had written-off all debts and stocks older than twelve months. They made it attractive for us to buy because they simply wanted out. Nobody wanted to catch a falling knife, except my brother and I. We decided to buy up the 85 per cent shares offered and to keep the company alive.

I mortgaged my house, and my wife emptied her life savings so that I could pay off the French partners. My brother did the same. We paid the French cash but asked Kenny and Nicholas for an eighteen-month instalment plan while I sought to raise more capital by liquidating stocks and collecting debts. They accepted our offer for old times' sake. My brother now owns 47.5 per cent of Besco, while I own 52.5 per cent since I decided to run the company alone thereafter.

Turnaround management is the highest level of mental stress and I felt I was losing the fight for the first time in my life. Each day, I imagined a white envelope on my table and wondered who was going to resign next. I even dreamt of that white envelope in my sleep. I felt like a failure each time somebody resigned because they lost confidence in me. I tried to use some of my coping mechanisms.

Instead of spending full time at the office, I spent 50 per cent of my time every day running the Restroom Association, which I started in 1998, and the World Toilet Organization, which I founded in 2001. My staff asked me how I could waste half my time running charities while turning around a troubled business. I told them that the social work energized me and allowed me to survive the recession. If I'd stayed in the office full time, I might have ended up having a mental breakdown.

Mental illness can hit anyone. At forty, I was having a great run with sixteen profitable businesses, and suddenly I lost half of all that money. It didn't matter that half the money was still a lot of money.

I felt a sense of worthlessness, perhaps due to withdrawal symptoms stemming from my addiction to successes in the last sixteen years. A feeling that I was not clever any more. I used to see ideas and colourful pictures whenever I closed my eyes. Now everything was dismal, brown, and murky whenever I closed my eyes. Life was no longer beautiful. I was almost entering depression when I realized that my typically cheerful wife was beginning to stop smiling. I told myself that if both of us were depressed, the family would be screwed and the four little kids would be at a loss.

I was desperately looking for solutions when I found a hypnotherapist—Jennifer Norris-Nielsen of Grey Matter.

She helps sportsmen and women improve their performances through mental strength.

She interviewed me about my feelings and aspirations and took notes about my thoughts. She sat me down on the couch and I followed her voice bringing me into Alpha state meditation, a state of complete relaxation and passive attention. As I listened to the instructions of her voice, I immersed myself into an imaginary ocean and in my hypnotic state, she brought me through a fascinating journey inside my mind and rewired my thoughts at a subconscious level. Everything was imaginary as described by her voice. I visited a castle where I wrote my fears on a blackboard, then I erased it and wrote how I wish to feel positively. I closed the door of the castle and locked it. This became my new subconscious programming. I travelled to several such places that I cannot remember clearly now. I remember taking a lift to the top of a tower. I rearranged a messy bunch of wires and rewired them to the plug. In the process, I rewired myself. It was like a miracle. When I returned to full consciousness after two hours, I was full of love and I'd reverted to my happy self again. Jennifer was very satisfied with her success as well. Gone were my fears and anxieties. My mind was crystal clear, and I knew what I had to do. I went back to turn around the loss-making businesses to profit.

Jennifer told me if I suffered any relapse, I should visit her again. I didn't relapse. I was cured, and now I had a clear plan for the recovery of my company. I later learned that my hypnotherapy went well because of the complete trust I placed in Jennifer during the process. There was no holding back.

The first stop was to meet all my bankers. Besides the businesses, I owned fifteen properties at that time. My average loan was at 50 per cent of property value, which I thought was a very prudent and safe level. However, property prices plunged by nearly 50 per cent during that prolonged recession triggered by a series of events. The Asian Currencies Crisis in 1997 was followed by the dot-com crash in 2000 and the SARS virus crisis in 2003. The bankers were inundated with distressed properties. I told them to believe in me and not seize my properties. To ease my cash flow, I offered to pay them only the interest but not the instalments. They agreed to this arrangement for the next twelve months, with the option to review again thereafter.

My second stop was to visit all my debtors. They were delaying their payments to me in order to preserve their own cash flow. However, when I offered them a 20 per cent discount if they paid me cash immediately, many of them took my offer. In a recession, such deals could help them show increased profitability to their bankers. Since these debts were already written-off by my former partners, they were pure profits for me. Besco started to recover from its cash-tight situation.

My third action was to liquidate inventories and sell them at a 50 per cent discount. Stocks that had been over twelve months old were already written-off in our books when the partners sold me the shares. So again, the customers were very happy to snap up these basement bargains and we managed to get the cash to repay Kenny and Nicholas for the eighteen-month instalments. I also threw away lots of old things in the stores in order to establish a new order and clean discipline for the workers. When the spaces are cluttered, our minds are cluttered. When the spaces are clean, our minds are efficient and productive. This applies to everyone from the factory floor to the office. We painted the walls a bright yellow colour to reflect our optimism. We needed a new, brave spirit to face this crisis together.

I realized that when my mind was calm, everything was clearer and simpler to solve. When my mind was emotional, all kinds of unnecessary distractions caused me to lose focus on the solutions. The problems remained the same, but it was easier to solve them without anxiety.

Nevertheless, turnaround management is highly intense work. My head full of black hair actually turned partially white in the course of the six gruelling months.

In times of uncertainty, you may lose some money, but you must not lose your mind.

Here is another series of coping mechanisms I added to my toolkit:

1. Imagine the worst scenario that could happen and accept it. For example, I might fear becoming bankrupt, but if I accept that possibility courageously, my fear disappears. Fear of the unknown is often scarier than the known. By making the worst scenario specific and known, it is easier to confront it instead of worrying. Most often, the worst scenario does not happen.
2. Imagine the best scenario and accept it. This is an optimistic and happy scenario. By making this scenario concrete, it is easier to have hope in case it happens. Think about some 'what if' scenarios that can open up new possibilities. Most often, the best scenario does not happen. But it provides optimism and hope.
3. Imagine the 'most likely' scenario and accept it. This is a pragmatic scenario. By making this scenario concrete, I overcome my fear of the worst scenario and also my cravings for the best scenario.

Since you are able to accept all three scenarios, you may now reconcile your fears and have lower anxieties than before.

By 2005, all the companies were either profitable again or closed down or sold to other shareholders. I was left only with Besco, which owned a 3,000-square-metre factory and some minority shares in Maybricks. I sold ten properties to repay the bank loans and became debt-free with five properties remaining, of which I rented three, stayed in one, and had another one occupied by my mother and her maid. The rental income was enough to pay for our family's expenses and I reached a state of bliss. I didn't want to go back to the gambling table of businesses any more.

I told Julie that it makes no sense to be in the madness of the rat race. Instead, I decided that I'll do social work for the rest of my life. She told me happiness is worth much more than money.

Friends often asked me why I'd waste my time doing something that didn't make money. They didn't understand that if you've found your meaning in life, it is much more valuable than money.

I discovered that I could live in a light-hearted mode all the time. When my friends showed me their new cars, I congratulated them for their success, and yet I did not feel any need to compare myself with them. I accepted that the aspirations of others may be different from mine. I was able to defeat my jealousy.

Detachment from cravings for money, fame, power was a great cure for my soul.

The opposite of the word 'poor' is not 'rich'. It is 'sufficient'. Once I saw how money and the lack of it drove people to the extreme during the Asian Financial Crisis; I found that money didn't bring happiness. Caring for others brought happiness.

Lesson:

A good way to cope with challenges is to help others who are in trouble. When you are able to give love to others, it heals you as well. When you focus on your own problems, you're miserable. When you help others, you feel useful and are full of joy.

Aligning the World Inside
with the World Outside

The Difference Between Loving and Defending Myself

I used to feel the need to protect myself against others. I would see a potential threat and feel a need to defend against it. I would be constantly looking for enemies and be afraid of others.

When the other parties sensed my defensive position, they'd similarly put up their defence system to protect themselves. If you're afraid of me, I'll be afraid of you. Sometimes, such distrust leads to pre-emptive attacks and things get messy after that (very similar to why countries go to war).

This process generates a self-fulfilling mutual distrust, and also unnecessary internal stress, anxieties, and toxicity in your body.

Defensiveness is a fear-based activity. The better alternative is to love myself.

My solution is to simply imagine that everyone loves me by default. To be loved, I will need to be lovable. I accept myself for who I am and when I love myself as a very nice person, I start to see the goodness in others as well. When others see that I trust and love them, they'll similarly love me back. The good thing about this process is that I become unattractive to the fear-based people.

If I love them and if they can't accept it, they tend to move away.

I learned that I could love people this way as my default, unless proven otherwise.

By practising this daily, I realized that others are lovable too. To be clear, loving myself is not narcissism nor conceit. It is not condescending and does not depend on making others lesser or making myself larger. Loving myself is accepting myself, loving others is accepting others, warts and all. They are who they are, and they are lovable by default.

Securing Myself, Securing Others

Whenever you are in a plane, the flight safety briefing instructs you that in the case of an emergency, secure yourself first with a mask before you secure others. I see life in the same way. After you have secured your own oxygen mask, you should ensure others also have their oxygen masks. You cannot try to put on two oxygen masks or fifty, or buy up all the oxygen masks, because you don't need more than one mask. If there is a child or an elderly who doesn't know how to put on their oxygen mask, you should help them put on their mask. This is the way to help all passengers on a plane survive. And this is the same way we can help humanity survive.

As a child, I was made to feel secure when I was helped by my parents and relatives. I am grateful for their magnanimity in helping me grow from a vulnerable newborn to an independent adult. As an adult, I started securing myself financially by selling my time for money. When I attained financial independence, my time was priceless, and selling time to buy money became a loss-making business. Many people don't realize that making more money than needed is a loss-making business. They leave so much unspent and unused money at the time of their death, not realizing that these monies were paid with Time, the real currency of life. Unused money is useless at death.

So, what is the highest exchange value for time?

The answer I found personally is Service. I want to work for Purpose and Meaning.

Strangely, many millionaires and billionaires, who have already exceeded their requirement for financial independence, continue chasing money until they die. And they never get to use that extra money they earned.

I interviewed a billionaire once and asked him if he had time to spend his money. He said he was so busy making more money that he had no time to spend it. He said that when he died, his children would inherit his money. When I asked him if his children would spend it, he said he hoped not to spoil his children with his wealth. Then, why did he continue to make more and more money beyond his ability to use it? He told me that compared to those wealthier than him, he was actually not rich enough!

The root cause of this perceived wealth disparity is the way we give recognition to the rich and powerful. We teach our children that they must endeavour to be wealthy. We envy those who appear on *Forbes* or *Fortune* magazine's wealth rankings.

We mention the names of ultra-rich billionaires as if they're the role model we aspire to become.

In this process, we celebrate those who hoard wealth and deprive others of it. Inadvertently, we promote extreme selfishness and drive money to the apex of a few people. This is a game design that created rampant poverty. This is not about socialism, communism, capitalism, colonialism, or any other extreme philosophy. These extreme philosophies have not really worked sustainably so far. We need pragmatism to find our natural pathways to a joyful life.

I realized that I needed to rearrange my vocabulary of life:

1. Replace 'More' with 'Sufficient': I must decide what is enough and what is excessive. I choose to live moderately. Wealth, Fame, and Power are intoxicating, and they can consume me if I over-consume them.

2. Replace 'Power' with 'Balance': I use whatever influence I may have to create balance, social justice, and equity. I discovered that the superiority complex and inferiority complex are Siamese twins. I am not inferior or superior to others. I seek harmony and balance.

3. Replace 'Cravings' with 'Detachment': After leaving the rat race, I discovered that I could be detached from jealousy. I stopped comparing myself to others. I have enough and I am happy.

4. Replace 'Fear' with 'Compassion': When I focus on materialism, I am miserable and full of fear because I can feel my consciousness narrowing and choking me up. When I focus on giving love and service to others, I can feel my consciousness widening and making me joyful. I finally understand the meaning of having a big heart versus being narrow-minded.

5. Replace 'Anxiety' with 'Peace of Mind': When I crave, I suffer internal struggle, I feel heavy and negatively stressed. When I detach myself from cravings, I feel light, creative, and positively energized. Peace of mind is about accepting myself and devoting myself to serve others. I do not fear if I win or lose. When I want

nothing, I lose nothing. When I have nothing to lose, I am free from anxiety.

6. Replace 'Self' with 'Humanity': I try to practise Lao Tzu's teaching of Non-Self and Non-Action. Acting without force and going with the natural flow of things in harmony with others.

7. Replace 'Money' with 'Relevance': Instead of focusing on making more money for myself, I focus on making my existence more relevant to others. I am constantly conscious that time is the real currency of life and I need to cherish every opportunity to be useful.

Lessons:

Love yourself and understand that the definition of Purpose and Meaning is a personal choice. Think deeply and find your own answers.

Imagine what you'd like to say to yourself on the last day of your life. I don't think you'd want to check your bank balance in those last moments.

The Search for Meaning

My journey to philanthropy started just after the age of thirty when my businesses were stable. I eventually ended up retiring from the rat race completely by 2005. I wanted to be a more wholesome person not just a money-making machine. It was not a calculated decision. The feeling is simply a family tradition that giving back is good. It's like a useful hobby that is beneficial for others. It was the same thing my mother and my grandmother did. My grandmother organized the migration of her entire extended family from a little island in Indonesia to Singapore because she saw no future there for them. They'd stay in our house and the houses of others until they found jobs, wives, or husbands. We grew up with a strong sense of community.

Seeking Roots in Heritage Conservation

I started searching for something meaningful to help society. In 1989, the Urban Redevelopment Authority (URA) announced the conservation of Singapore's heritage buildings. I was very excited and joined the Singapore Heritage Society. There was so much to read about their architectural significance and history. I learned about how the air well provides natural ventilation that keeps the houses cool without needing air conditioning, and how each period brought new styles of architecture with influences from British, French, Malay, Chinese, and Indian cultures. Each house is so beautiful even when they look old and broken. I started buying old shophouses in Singapore and restoring them to rent out. I was also fascinated by those in the other Straits Settlements in Penang and Melaka.

One day, Julie and I were touring the old town of Melaka. I was so nostalgic for the old-world charm that when Julie said she loved these houses, I immediately bought one on impulse. It was a dilapidated 13,000 square feet heritage house at 70 Heeren Street. It cost 260,000 ringgit to buy and 800,000 ringgit to restore. I later named it Malaqa House and it was given the status of an official museum. I bought a dilapidated colonial bungalow for my family house and restored it to its former old-world charm. However, buying and restoring old heritage buildings became too expensive for a hobby. There was a limit to the amount of money I could borrow from the bank and I did not want to be over leveraged. I decided to find another cause to serve.

Samaritans of Singapore

I had to look for something else, some more meaningful thing to do, so I volunteered at the Samaritans of Singapore (SOS), a distress anonymous call service with a holistic approach to suicide prevention, intervention, and postvention.

There were twenty volunteers in our cohort of counselling trainees. We were trained in active listening and empathy. We learned not to impose our own values onto the callers. It took nine months of weekly training to prepare us for how to handle each type of call. The success rate was very low.

I learned a lot about active listening, how to stay calm, detached, caring, and empathetic. We were not allowed to suggest or recommend solutions. We were not allowed to use our real names. I used 'Alfred' as my pseudonym. Most importantly, we were not allowed personal contact with the client. For example, if a girl was sad about a break-up with a boyfriend, we could not tell her that the ocean is full of fishes and she can easily find another guy. That would trivialize her feelings and alienate her. Only six of us graduated from the course and were allowed to go on the phones without supervision.

Through this volunteer work, I learned about the ills of our society, how most pains were self-inflicted, how narrow-mindedness closes out options for solutions, and how common mental illness was prevalent in many people. For example, when a man loses his job and he starts drinking to drown his sorrow, he might end up drunk, beating his wife, or getting into a car accident. I learned that if I have one problem, I must not let emotions add a second problem, which might lead to a series of unintended new problems. My job was to feel their pains through empathy and to guide them into finding solutions. After each successful session, the caller would thank me for all my advice, when in fact I never offered any. All the 'advice' was generated by the caller themself. This is the power of active listening.

If someone said they felt like committing suicide, I'd ask them what their other options were and let them evaluate these options themselves. The truth was that people who called the SOS didn't want to die. They needed someone to talk to.

After a while, I felt that serving one person at a time (during the call) was not scalable in terms of impact. There were so few of us and the other phones kept ringing while we were busy attending to calls. The nature of our work dictated that we could not end the call abruptly. We even had to attend to prank calls from mental patients who refused to take their medicines.

After eighteen months, I left SOS feeling that I needed to serve a larger impact, as personalized services are not scalable.

Lessons:

There are financial limits to the things you can own. You can't buy them all.

Listening skills and empathy can help others figure out their own solutions. Do not indulge your personal value systems onto the other person by prescribing your solutions. Help them decide for themselves.

Helping one person or restoring one house is not scalable. Think of solutions that are more scalable using system change.

BECOMING MR TOILET

Turning the 007 upside down to make LOO

Restroom Association of Singapore

In 1996, I was looking for the next big problem to solve when I read in the morning newspaper about our then Prime Minister Goh Chok Tong saying: 'I have chosen cleanliness of public toilets as a marker because firstly, public toilets are common properties, and secondly, their state of cleanliness reflects our considerateness for others'. I thought I should take up this challenge since it was a grossly neglected problem. The government had been unsuccessful so far in delivering clean toilets. They were blaming the public and I felt the answer lay in the users, facilities owners, cleaners, and policies.

I registered with the Restroom Association of Singapore and declared that I would solve the dirty toilet problems in Singapore. Both the English and Mandarin mainstream media gave me front page coverage. Many Singaporeans said someone ought to have started this long ago. The public's support was enthusiastic. But when I went to meet Daniel Wang Nan Jee, the Director-General of the National Environment Agency (NEA), he told me:

'Jack, this is a hopeless effort despite your good intentions. I've tried the last twenty years and people behave so badly in toilets; nothing can change.'

I went away unperturbed. I bought a fountain pen and wrote him a hand-written letter:

Dear Daniel,

No matter how your children misbehave, you will always love them and try new ways until things work out well.

You are the Father of Toilets for Singaporeans. Do not give up on your 'children' and I will be there to help you make Public Toilets Clean in Singapore.

I believe we can succeed.

He was personally touched. He organized a whole government meeting with all the government agencies including the People's Association (PA), National Parks, NEA, Sports Council, and the Ministry of Education. Everyone agreed that I should develop a roadmap and I went forward to create the ABC workplan:

Architecture, Behaviour, and Cleaning

Architecture: If the restroom is designed to be dry and easy to clean, it needs to ergonomically follow the natural time and motion workflow of the users. Lighting, ventilation, visual experience, signage for pathfinding, and loos-caping need to uplift the user's experience. For example, at the basin, wetting of hands, soap supply, washing and drying of hands must be all at the same place. If paper napkins are used, a disposal hole is needed directly under the dried hands. Designs have to facilitate ease of access to nooks and crevices for cleaning, therefore we need to minimize any spaces that might retain dirt or wetness.

Behaviour: If the design and cleaning is good, the users will feel cared for and their behaviour will also be good. If the restroom respects the users, the users will respect the toilet.

Cleaning: Cleaners have to be professionally trained as Hygiene Officers. Cleaners should be full of pride, understanding that their work contributes to public health daily and prevents widespread illnesses.

I persuaded the shopping malls that they could increase their revenue through customer retention and increased foot traffic if their toilets were clean and shoppers didn't have to leave their buildings when they needed to use the toilets. They agreed and started cleaning up. Today, our shopping malls compete to use their toilets as part of their customer service.

I have four kids in school, and they have lots of cousins and friends. They all told me toilets in school stink. I went to schools and educated the principals that many students held their bladders throughout the school day because the school toilets were dark and smelly. This was detrimental to their health, and it also affected their school results since their concentration in class was compromised by the discomfort in their bladders. The principals got the message and cleaned up. Schools' toilets are now professionally cleaned.

After one year, the NEA started funding the Restroom Association of Singapore annually until today. An advertising agency Dentsu Young & Rubicam designed our R(A) logo, which was our tongue-in-cheek parallel to the movie rating Restricted (Artistic) acronym.

Daniel Wang also cajoled Minister Lim Swee Say to open our inaugural World Toilet Summit on 19 November in 2001, a summit that attracted government agencies from fifteen countries as well. That day, 19 November, eventually became adopted by the UN General Assembly as the official UN World Toilet Day thirteen years later.

Minister Lim Swee Say continued to support our work when he was moved to the National Trade Union Congress (NTUC) where he funded our first World Toilet College to train toilet cleaners professionally.

Lesson:

Finding bureaucrats who believe in you is not easy. Just remember that bureaucrats are also people, and they also have a heart. Most of the time, it is the system that prevents them from action. If you can touch their hearts, maybe you can motivate them.

The Dark Stain on the Country

In 2023, a survey report by Singapore Management University (SMU) revealed that 66.74 per cent of Singaporeans said public toilets in hawker centres and coffee shops remain as dirty as they were three years ago, or 'have become much dirtier' than the previous two surveys done in 2020 and 2016.[6] All data produced by their three surveys in eight years were ignored by our National Environment Agency and the Singapore Food Agency, despite their invitation for them to use their reports in 2016 and 2020.

In the 2023 survey, 60 per cent of respondents said that efforts in cleaning up toilets in hawker centres and coffee shops were ineffective; only 6 per cent of Singaporeans were optimistic about the efficacy of clean toilet campaigns.

Most of Singapore's 1,200 coffee shops and 119 hawker centres neither supply proper soap nor toilet paper even though most Singaporeans eat daily at coffee shops and hawker centres. The public is disgusted by these dirty toilets, so they seldom use them. However, what they do not realize is that the cooks and food preparation staff at these places also use the toilet there. Therefore, if they washed their hands only with water and diluted soap that has no viscosity, they would prepare food with those dirty hands, and the faecal materials might end up in the food served to their customers. To make things worse, the SMU survey also showed many food preparations on the floor next to these dirty toilets!

It is sad to see that people would resist visiting such toilets, and yet readily or unwittingly eat the cook's dirt without knowing. One gram of faeces can contain 10 million viruses and 1 million bacteria, 1,000 parasite cysts, and 100 parasite eggs.[7] That is why it is so dangerous.

I thought that since I could succeed in persuading shopping centres to clean up their toilets, I could do the same with the coffee shop owners, but this time I failed. They told me that since they offer the cheapest food in Singapore, dirty toilets would not affect their business as all diners already know that their toilets are dirty, and few actually use them. They reasoned that if they kept the toilets clean, many people would use them and this would incur extra costs on water bills, soap, toilet paper, and cleaning services.

To date, these coffee shop toilets remain a dark stain on Singapore's image as a clean and green garden city.

The Singapore government's first Clean Toilet Campaign started in 1983, and the government has been blaming the users for the last forty years, but it hasn't worked. Here's why:

1. There will always be a very small number of recalcitrants who mess up. They may litter or spill but because there are no cameras inside the toilets, it is impossible to enforce punishment on them.
2. There are those who cannot control themselves. There are those who are visually impaired, those with dementia,

Alzheimer's, Parkinson's disease, and incontinence in an increasingly ageing population.

3. Even the ordinary person may have occasional bouts of diarrhoea that may cause their bodily discharge to splatter all over the toilet bowl. Our low water flushing system may not be able to wash the entire surface of the bowl, especially the upper surface, to properly clear the shit. These situations require the cleaners to clean up.

4. All our public toilets have a mandatory sensor operated auto-flush system. If it is not maintained properly, it cannot flush. This is caused by poor maintenance, which is the responsibility of the owners. We cannot blame the users for not flushing an auto-flush toilet that does not work. Yet, our NEA's posters keep reminding the users to flush the toilet, forgetting that it's auto-flush.

5. A toilet does not clean itself. Unlike littering, a toilet does not clean itself if there are no cleaners. We deposit our bodily waste into toilets; therefore, toilets will be dirty within a few hours. Urine and faeces are dirt that produce smell. So, daily cleaners are needed.

6. If a public toilet with heavy usage is not deeply scrubbed in a few months, it will have ammonia and dirt deposits in the WC, urinals, and on the floor and walls.

The users of the shopping centres and coffee shops are the same people. If the shopping centre toilets can be kept clean while the coffee shops' toilets are dirty, the difference is the owners' attitude and not the users.

From 2020 to 2022 the NEA offered a 90 per cent grant for the coffee shop owners to renovate their toilets, and only 38 out of 1,200 coffee shops had applied for the grant as of August 2021.[8] It is clear that they preferred to keep their toilets dirty and in poor conditions to discourage usage of their toilets. To give you an idea of the profitability of a coffee shop: a few coffee shops have been sold for above SGD 40 million each. Yet, they stinge on even providing liquid soap in toilets for handwashing, many dilute the liquid soap with water such that they do not have the viscosity to soap up your hands.

Enforcement of fines and foreclosures are the only solutions. Singapore has been so well-known for implementing fines that we are called a Fine Country. We have to slap penalties on the owners for their negligence. There are no other financial models for keeping toilets clean, unless the public demands for cleanliness the same way the Japanese people demand for it.

The public should continuously demand and pressure the government to act. Once this becomes a political challenge and it affects the electoral votes, I am sure the problem will be solved very expeditiously.

After Minister Lim Swee Say left the Ministry of Environment in 2005, there has been one senior politician who seems very protective of the coffee shop owners since taking office in 2006. Enforcements against these owners have been particularly lax. Although the Singapore Management University's survey showed that no improvement in the 1,200 coffee shops' toilets were marked as dirty, there were only about 400 fines issued by the Singapore Food Authority (SFA) per year. Each fine is only about SGD 400. The coffee shop owners can easily do their sums as follows: Keeping their toilets clean costs about SGD 2,000 a month or SGD 24,000 per year. Getting fined once a year is only SGD 400. They can easily save SGD 23,600 a year by keeping their toilets dirty! And the chance of getting fined is only 33 per cent. This is the reason their toilets are deliberately dirty!

Coffee shops and hawker centres are the last frontiers we need to conquer before every Singaporean can be proud to call Singapore a clean, green, and liveable city, complete with clean toilets nationwide.

In 2024, as our Prime Minister Lee Hsien Loong hands over leadership to the new Prime Minister Mr Lawrence Wong, I wrote to our Prime Minister Lee Hsien Loong to request that he treats toilet cleanliness as his last legacy before handing over the leadership of the government to a new incoming Prime Minister. He forwarded my request to a new team at NEA and SFA. I met Senior Parliamentary Secretary Baey Yam Keng, the Deputy CEO of NEA, and the Deputy CEO of SFA, together with their respective officers. We had a very frank discussion and they finally agreed on a vision of 100 per cent clean public toilets in the whole of Singapore. They agreed that to be effective, enforcement must include suspension of the coffee shops' operations after repeat fines. They also agreed to make these fines and suspensions highly visible so as to mobilize the public to demand cleanliness of all toilets. In this way, we would be able to stop blaming the users and convert them into positive drivers for toilet cleanliness from the owners. Finally, the new team appreciated the alignment of our mutual mission and I was welcomed back as a friend after eighteen years!

As of writing this book, this is still work-in-progress. The Ministry of Sustainability and Environment has declared 2024 as the Year of Public Hygiene, and a Public Toilet Taskforce is now established to look into solving the dirty toilet challenges in Singapore.[9] I hope they will do what they promised to do. I'll continue to monitor and motivate them to do a better job.

I've brought eleven experts from the Taiwan Toilet Association to brief them on how the Taiwanese and Japanese keep their toilets clean. I'm now creating a toilet app similar to TripAdvisor, for the public to post their reviews of the clean and dirty toilets in Singapore to help the diners avoid eating at dirty places. I'm also inviting the Japanese trainers to come to Singapore to train Singaporean trainees and toilet cleaners.

Lesson:

Sometimes, it is hard to fight a powerful politician who is still in office. Be patient. Monitor and wait for the window of opportunity to open, and then take action. The wait can take years. It can be frustrating, but if you wait long enough, the opportunity will arrive eventually.

Asia-Pacific Toilet Symposium at Kitakyushu 1999

The Birth of World Toilet Organization

After I founded the Restroom Association of Singapore in 1998, I discovered there was a Japan Toilet Association in Tokyo. I joined their Asia-Pacific Toilet Symposium in Kitakyushu, Japan, in 1999. I was so happy to discover that there were fifteen toilet associations in the world. Those present were from Japan, the USA, Thailand, Cambodia, Malaysia, Sweden, Norway, Korea, Nepal, Singapore, Taiwan, UK, India, and Vietnam.

We learned how the Japanese toilet culture began at home with the belief that 'your toilet is your face'. Visitors to your home will inevitably visit your toilet and they may form an impression of your family upbringing according to the cleanliness and tidiness of your home toilet. The need to avoid embarrassment became a major driver for the clean toilet culture.

In schools, children were taught to take responsibility to clean up their school toilets, to be considerate, and not to mess up. Their schools' toilets were so clean and dry that they could sit on the floor of the toilet and have picnics.

This same toilet culture was even more stringent at their workplaces. Customers were known to cancel orders when they visited factories with dirty toilets that signified the poor discipline in production culture and a risk of defective or imperfect products. The message was simple: If you don't have diligence to keep a simple toilet clean, how can you run a company in harmony with the pride of your workers who are required to produce products they can be proud of?

Sanitation has clearly been a non-charismatic agenda as donors, foreign aid funding, and corporation sponsorship monies always go to water instead of sanitation. Like an orphan, sanitation has always been parked under the Water Agenda and the development sector has long treated sanitation as the ugly duckling, with water as the swan.

Sanitation and hygiene provide dignity, health, and safety, particularly among women and girls. When public toilets are inaccessible or not secure, women are at a higher risk of harassment. Access to safe and clean toilets also helps adolescent girls stay in school; they have to drop out of schools when there is no toilet available with the privacy to change sanitary napkins. When girls and women go out in the open to defecate alone, they subject themselves to the risk of peeping toms, molestation, rape, and even murder when rapists want to destroy evidence of their crime.

The loss of tourism income and pollution of rivers and clean water by defaecation are also enormous negative externalities, but such public goods are often badly managed by incompetent governments.

While some may think it is rude to discuss toilets, we have to tear down the stigma around toilets in order to save lives.

Ultimately, getting the message across is of utmost importance because the consequences of proper sanitation are very far-reaching, impacting health, the environment, safety, and even education.

I was determined to break this taboo and end this social injustice. The problem was so untenable that I wanted to own the problem.

Although our discussions at Asia-Pacific Toilet Symposium were very passionate and the facts were mind-blowing, I was worried that this may end up as another talk shop without legacy, if we didn't get into implementation mode after we dispersed at the end of the meeting. I felt that we needed to create an organized global movement to address Toilets and Sanitation openly and widely. I asked the Japanese to lead the formation of a global toilet body, but they declined because they said that they didn't speak English fluently and this initiative would require effective communication. Instead, everyone asked me to lead, and so I agreed to form a world body. Thus, the World Toilet Organization was created, with me as its leader and primary advocate. I also promised them that I'd host a World Toilet Summit in 2001 in Singapore and that it would be professionally managed with global media coverage on the sanitation crisis. This was the start of my exhilarating journey in the toilet world.

Lessons:

Think with a system-change mindset, when solving large-scale problems.

Observe the patterns of fragmented resources that you can orchestrate into a synergised network mutually empowering each other.

When a window of opportunity arises, seize it before it is closed or taken by others.

Offer yourself for leadership roles where none are willing.

With Mechai, Mr Condom

The Power of Humour

I was a novice in the social development sector at the international level. I wanted to leapfrog my learning and also avoid making all kinds of beginner's mistakes. I was impressed and inspired by Mr Condom's success in promoting the use of condoms in Thailand, so I called up my friend in Bangkok's Sewerage Department and asked her to help make an appointment to meet him.

His real name is Mechai Viravaidya, and his advocacy has been so successful that he saved millions from sexually transmitted diseases, unplanned parenthood, and abortions.

Yet, he succeeded by making a fool of himself blowing balloons with condoms and teaching the girls in brothels and massage parlours that 'Condom is a Girl's Best Friend'. He even got the Thai mafia involved to promote the 'No Condom, No Sex' policy across the prostitution industry. He convinced them by telling them that healthy workers are more profitable than sick ones. He told me as long as they help save the girls from diseases and unplanned pregnancies, it doesn't matter who they are.

I was totally amazed by his audacity and the creativity in his approaches. He didn't care about his own image, he only wanted to save lives.

We met at his Condom and Cabbages Restaurant in Bangkok, a popular social business that raises awareness of safe sex with contraceptives. I asked him what mindset was needed for me to build the World Toilet Organization.

He asked me, 'Can you make people laugh?'

I replied, 'Yes. I'm a joker by nature.'

He told me, 'People will laugh at you and when they do, don't be upset. When they laugh at you, they're listening to you. Remember this.'

This lesson was an eye-opener for me because it clarified for me what I need to do to strengthen my resilience. The strategy perfectly fits my 'naughty boy, artist, and joker' self-image. I can be defiant, making a fool of myself without any apprehension or self-doubt, while doing good at the same time.

That was how I created the WTO pun on the World Trade Organization by calling ourselves the other WTO. I was willing to take risk for the greater good, like Mechai did. Afterall, the downside was very low, as nobody would sue a new, penniless non-profit for money. I imagined that if the World Trade Organization decided to sue me, their first step would be a cease-and-desist warning letter, and all I would owe is an apology.

Anyways, providence would have it that they did not sue me and we became well-known as The Other WTO.

I wanted to design the WTO logo myself. I tried to think of a universal image. It had to be minimalistic to be as lasting as the Red Cross logo, or the Nike's swoosh. It had to create instant love of the toilet and sanitation. And it must be elegant enough to be able to remove the taboo surrounding the topic.

The day I designed the logo, I started out in a standing position looking down at my WC for a very long time without inspiration. Then I sat down on the floor to rest. At that angle, I saw the potential of the toilet seat cover as a heart shape.

I designed a blue heart-shaped toilet seat cover as our logo: Love Your Toilet.

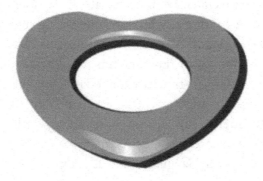

In 2006, at the Davos, World Economic Forum, a Director of Publicis who was organizing the public relations work at the forum told me his experience encountering our WTO brand. He was having breakfast at home when he read about the World Toilet Organization in a Swiss newspaper. He remembered that his first reaction was that this organization has the wrong name. Who is going to believe an entity with the word 'Toilet' inside its name? Then, three hours later at his office, it suddenly dawned on him that WTO was a brilliant brand! He told me that the name stuck in his head for three hours, and a brand that is that sticky is very powerful. Because people remember bizarre names better, the World Toilet Organization, or WTO, is a brand that will indelibly be etched in the reader's memory forever after the first encounter!

How to Build a Guerrilla Brand

1. **Be authentic.** Don't fake a story. Tell it from the heart. No need to quote others. Tell your own stories with feeling.
2. **Be audacious.** Don't worry about naysayers. Focus on the real audience who will benefit from your story.
3. **Be original.** Tell it fresh each time, even if you have told the same story a thousand times. Tell it like you're telling it for the first time, accommodating for the cultural or interest contexts of the new audience.
4. **Be energized.** Passion and energy will transcend the audience. Your body language speaks volumes so non-verbal language is as important as verbal cues spoken.
5. **Be concise.** Use lots of soundbites and help create punchy headlines for the interviewer. The editor will have to vet the story and if it was told before, he might not run it. Make sure you create news angles for the journalist.
6. **Call a spade a spade.** Sincerity and authenticity are highly appreciated. Speak the truth without reservation. Believe that you'll always be forgiven for doing good.
7. **Focus on the message and not on yourself.** Your mission is paramount, it's much larger than you. If you try to be famous, you'll immediately become repulsive. Self-promotion is a major turn-off for any audience.
8. **Sacrifice for the story.** War journalists get killed in crossfire telling their stories in war zones. I may look

irreverent in quirky shots, but the impact of the story is more important than me. Think about the mission rather than thinking about yourself.

9. **Push is expensive and Pull is free.** I've never spent money on media. Our outreach is in the billions for worldwide audiences annually. I can't go to the people, but my stories can bring people to support me. I may get rejections if I knock on the wrong doors. But if they come to me, it would save lots of time (and money).

10. **Use humour appropriately.** Humour has been working for me for twenty-seven years now. It may seem risky in a politically correct world, but there is respect for courage in humour if you can play at the edge but not fall off the cliff into vulgarities. I've developed a unique blend of humour and serious facts that stays elegant and appealing. The WTO remains highly respected all over the world.

Lesson:

Bizarre is Sticky. Once a person is exposed to World Toilet Organization's branding, it becomes indelibly etched in their mind forever, and we become the first thing they recall whenever they engage with topics relating to toilets and sanitation.

Left to Right: Edward Liu, Daniel Wang,
Minister Lim Swee Say, Jack Sim

World Toilet Summit 2001

After promising the group in Japan in 1999, I wanted a big impact for our inaugural World Toilet Summit, but such a meeting could easily cost more than a hundred thousand dollars in venue and management costs.

Then I remembered a book I had read during my school days, *Tom Sawyer* by Mark Twain. Tom Sawyer was a mischievous boy with a pure heart. One day, he was punished by Aunt Polly to whitewash her fence on a Sunday. He didn't want to do it and instead convinced several boys that the extremely unpleasant task was actually a fun project. He made the work seem extremely absorbing. In this way, Tom actually convinced them to paint the fence, and even got them to barter things like marbles and firecrackers for the privilege of doing so. Aunt Polly was so impressed that she made supper for Tom. This American classic exemplified the leverage model. I applied the lessons I'd learned and believed that I could emulate Tom by motivating my friends to engage in this 'fun' project, hence getting my conference done for free.

I met with Edward Liu, owner of Conference and Exhibition Management Services. He had an upcoming Building Material Exhibition at the Singapore Expo in November 2001. I knew Edward was a public figure who cared about social issues and I also volunteered under his leadership in our neighbourhood's residence committee. We were both in the construction industry and it wasn't a cold call when I approached him for a barter trade. I told him I was trying to start a sanitation movement to address this neglected agenda. Since the conference room at the Singapore Expo will be empty after his opening ceremony, I asked him if he could let me use it for our two-day World Toilet Summit at no cost. He generously offered that if I sold sixteen exhibition booths for him, he would barter that for my World Toilet Summit, including giving me a press conference thrown in. We made the deal and I called all my friends in the construction industry to promote his show. I sold sixteen booths for him and he gave me a professionally managed first World Toilet Summit at absolutely zero cost!

The Singapore Minister for the Environment Lim Swee Say was the guest of honour, giving his opening address to government and association representatives from fifteen countries. Our inaugural World Toilet Summit was an overnight sensation. Never in my wildest dreams did I imagine that we would get media coverage from global news correspondents like Associated Press, Reuters, Asahi Shimbun, Yomiuri Shimbun, CNN, BBC, Xin Hua Press, Deutsche Presse-Agentur, Press Trust of India, APC, and *Wired* Magazine, but they came. Even TV stations worldwide, tabloids, and magazines covered our event. Edward was so impressed that he gave WTO a donation of SGD 8,000 as our first ever funder.

Clearly, I'd struck gold in the media arena by speaking the unspeakable; a subject that was suppressed for so long now 'exploded' on the media centre stage.

The electronic pagers of all the delegates were beeping and they received messages from their families and offices telling them that they saw them on TV (at that time, cell phones were not yet popular). Immediately, I'd created demand and had takers for the next three years, requesting to host the next series of our World Toilet Summit. Korea took 2002, India wanted 2003, and Beijing committed to host the 2004 summit.

And, I didn't have to sell exhibition booths any more.

Lessons:

Mutual Exploitation is Collaboration.
Collective Selfishness is Selflessness.
Make yourself useful to others and they can be useful to you.

Delegates at WTS 2002

World Toilet Summit 2002

The year 2002 was the year the World Cup was jointly hosted by Japan and Korea. One of the venues was the Suwon Football Stadium. It was also the year of re-election for the Mayor in Suwon City.

That year, our member, the Korean Clean Toilet Association, offered to host the 2002 World Toilet Summit and I gave them the hosting rights. But when I saw the announcement of the event, I was very surprised to see our World Toilet Summit being referred to as the inaugural World Toilet Association summit. I emailed to point out this typo but did not receive any reply. When one of the representatives told me that the event would be used to launch the re-election campaign for mayorship, I realized that this was a hijack to convert the WTO into WTA. Our social mission was being abused for personal political adventures. All my effort would be wasted if WTA replaced WTO through this trickery. I wrote an email that if the name was not changed back to WTO, I'd write an official letter addressed to the President of the Republic of Korea and meet the Korean Ambassador to Singapore to lodge an official complaint.

This time, the reply was immediate, suggesting a compromise: It will not be called a WTA event and the World Toilet Summit would proceed as planned. However, all the members would have to vote at the summit whether to retain the name World Toilet Organization or change it to World Toilet Association.

At the summit, every other member voted to retain the WTO's name since it was already famous with so much media publicity. I was very glad with the members' support and we continued as WTO. The summit went very well and the Korean public was very glad with the promotion of clean toilets in Korea.

I also discovered multiple benefits for the host of World Toilet Summit series:

1. **Media:** The World Toilet Summit series leveraged on its power to attract global media worth tens of millions of dollars or more each time, which made good investments of USD 300k to 500k sponsorship for each summit.

2. **Convening Power:** The WTO had massive convening power of stakeholders across different ares of expertise, geographies, and cultures. The awareness often shocked the audience and readers who never knew about the sanitation crisis. It created policy influences and triggered actions by governments, corporations, UN agencies, academia, philanthropists, civil societies, technologists, and local communities worldwide.

3. **Legacy:** Each summit left behind a lasting legacy of real change and impact on the local needs. We are a

mission-driven movement on a global scale but we
address challenges in local contexts.

Reflecting back on this incident, I was bold enough to threaten
him with a letter to the President of the Republic of Korea.
I was a novice challenging a veteran politician in his game.
I was glad that David defeated Goliath with a slingshot. He
also lost his mayoral seat to the Chairman of the Suwon City
Football Club and disappeared from our fraternity until 2006.

Lessons:

Social work can become political. Stay composed but stay firm.
Do not get angry, get even.

Someone may see you as powerless, but your power may lie
in your tenacity and your authenticity.

Cheating is a weakness and honesty is a strength.

World Toilet Summit 2003

In November 2002, SARS, the severe acute respiratory syndrome, broke out in the Guangdong province of China, and the World Health Organization issued a global alert in March 2003 as SARS spread widely. Dr Bindeshwar Pathak was preparing for the World Toilet Summit but he had to cancel it for safety reasons. SARS subsided after eight months and was declared as contained by WHO on 5 July 2003. The Taiwan Toilet Association offered to host the World Toilet Summit on 19 November. They brought the Deputy Mayor of Taipei to open our summit, which was attended mostly by Asian countries.

Since Beijing would be the host for next year's summit, I decided to use the Taiwan summit as a diplomatic bridge between Taiwan and Mainland China. I reasoned that if the US President Nixon could successfully use ping-pong as a soft-power to bridge the relationship with China, Toilets could also be such a soft power.

I invited a large delegation from Beijing to join the event. This included officials from the Beijing Tourism Bureau,

China Tourism Bureau, the People's Government of Beijing Municipality, Beijing Municipality Environmental Protection Bureau, and the Beijing Olympic Committee. Initially, there was apprehension between the Communists and the Taiwanese. But as they exchanged ideas, eating and drinking together, they started helping each other with solutions. I observed them building camaraderie, overcoming their political differences, and sharing common identity.

Indeed, they became good friends and as a return for the favour, a big delegation from Taiwan joined the 2004 World Toilet Summit in Beijing the following year.

Lesson:

Humans are social creatures and face-to-face meetings are critical. Relationships can be improved if people eat together, exchange cultures, and negotiate alliances respectfully. It can be a simple smile or a bow or an acknowledgement that one's views are heard. Trust is established when body languages communicate goodwill.

Toilet as a Soft Power

When Beijing was preparing for the 2008 Beijing Olympics Games, the Director of Beijing Municipality Tourism Bureau, Mr Yu Changjiang, had the enormous task of ensuring that all participants and visitors of the Beijing Olympics brought back positive memories of Beijing. While they knew they could put up a spectacular event, they were very worried about the embarrassing condition of public toilets in Beijing and the poor hygiene behaviour of their people. A major cultural transformation was needed to bring Beijing's tourist toilets up to world class level of cleanliness.

Given that the World Toilet Organization had been Singapore's de facto 'Toilet Foreign Affairs Department' since 2001, Mr Yu decided to host our World Toilet Summit 2004 to reassure the world that Beijing would be ready to welcome them for the Beijing Olympics 2008 in the most pleasant way.

My role was to bring all the experts to the summit, as well as frame the narratives for the global journalists and help prepare a strategy to implement this urgently needed transformation in Chinese toilet culture.

At the World Toilet Summit 2004, we renovated the Tiananmen Square's public toilets into a very pristine condition and even held a press conference inside the huge toilet. When I was asked by a journalist what I thought about the toilet conditions in China, I guess they were expecting a negative image of the current situation.

I replied that a journey of a thousand miles starts with the first step and the beautiful Tiananmen public toilet is the first step, a model for all China's tourist toilets in the future. The media reported very positively looking into the future of clean toilets in China instead of focusing on the unsightly status quo.

'Toilets represent the level of development of a country,' said Mr Yu, who was very pleased with the global coverage. He told me this was the cheapest media advertising campaign in his whole career. Our ability to mobilize editorial reports cost nothing and was much more credible than paid advertising. He never imagined being able to reach audiences from America, Europe, Japan, India, Russia, Africa, and the Association of Southeast Asian Nations (ASEAN), in one fell swoop.

The 2008 Beijing Olympics was one of the best shows to date in the Olympics' history, and thanks to clean toilets, there was absolutely no mention of the state of sanitation.

It turned out that my prediction in 2004 was true. After the success of Beijing's clean tourist toilets, China's tourism bureaus in every province, city, and county started cleaning up their act as they understood our mantra 'Better Toilets, More Tourists'. Our World Toilet Summit's legacy instilled in everyone a new mindset: Toilet equals profits.

As the Chinese accepted us as a friend, Shanghai, Macau, Xian, and Hainan also hosted our events, each leaving a legacy behind. By 2019, all tourist toilets in China from first-, second-, and third-tier cities were immaculately clean to national standards. This was a major toilet cultural revolution if we look back from 2004 when we started preparing for the Beijing Olympics.

Lesson:

Toilet is an invisible soft power. It is needed by everyone. It can be a bridge between so many nexuses from diplomacy and country branding to sports, health, education, gender equality, culture, transportation, tourism, and the environment.

I hope more governments can use this soft power seriously for bilateral and multilateral relationships.

Traditional 'Han' dry toilets without privacy,
poor hygiene with flies everywhere

Rainbow School Toilet Programme in China

After our 2004 World Toilet Summit and the subsequent success of the 2008 Beijing Olympics, all tourism bureaus in Chinese cities and provinces started to clean up their toilets to increase their tourism revenue. In the year 2015, the momentum accelerated when President Xi Jinping started the 'China Toilet Revolution' for the improvement of sanitation and hygiene in all of China. Aware of the outdated 'Han' sanitation systems still being used in rural parts of China, he addressed these issues by enacting long-lasting behavioural regulatory changes in rural homes and schools.

Prior to this, I had experienced a similar problem back home in Singapore. My four kids would tell me that they tried not to use the smelly school toilets and would only go once they reached home. I conducted a wider survey of kids from various schools in Singapore and they told me they had similar experiences. I reported the issue to the then Minister of Education, Tharman Shanmugaratnam. He referred me to the relevant officers in his ministry. They told me that if I said their toilets were clean and

I was helping them improve, they'd work with me. But if I said the toilets were smelly, they'd not work with me. I wrote back cc'ing to Tharman, and within one hour, a senior officer called me to tell me I should approach the individual schools myself as their survey showed that all their toilets were clean. I went to a series of schools and told the principals that when students hold their bladder in class, academic results suffer because their ability to concentrate is reduced. This message aligned their key performance with the toilets' cleanliness. I successfully persuaded them, egging them to hire professional cleaners for their schools. I was ready to do the same thing in China.

As I was trying to kickstart my work with the China Toilet Revolution, I received a call from Mr Victor Lim, who was my former manager in Diethelm. I was so happy to hear from him after thirty-five years! He and his business partner, Mr Khong, had been reading about my work and they said they'd like to donate some money for any project in China. Between 2016 and 2018, they supported the construction of fifteen schools, which benefited about 11,000 students in Luoyang County in Henan province, China. We trained the students to take ownership of their Rainbow School Toilets and clean them by rotating duty roster. This method also created a very conscientious behaviour as the students encouraged each other to keep it clean.

Here's what the students said:

'The toilets in our school used to be stinky, especially in summer when there are many flies and bugs. What scares me most is that sometimes small white bugs crawl out of the dung hole. It climbed onto my shoes several times. It's so disgusting! I don't like going to the toilet in school very much. When I returned to school, I saw a beautiful toilet. After going to the toilet, you can flush and wash your hands! I am very happy and love my new school toilet!'

'Now that we have clean flushing toilets, we felt we are now equal to the children in the big cities. It made us proud of ourselves.'

We gave our Rainbow School Toilet Model to the China's Ministry of Education for implementation in 215,000 schools in China. President Xi's China Toilet Revolution is now moving into rural schools and homes at a major scale.

Rainbow School Toilet

Training the children to handwash with soap

The girls love their new toilets

Students cleaning their own Rainbow School Toilet

Lessons:

Past connections may help you in the future when you least expect them to. Maintain friendly relationships with the people around you.

Donations can help you make a pilot, but the real scale happens when the local government takes over. Helping people solve their own problem is the only sustainable model.

With Prof Klaus Schwab and Hilde Schwab, the
co-founders of the World Economic Forum

At Davos, World Economic Forum

Joining the World Economic Forum (WEF)

My friend Lee Poh Wah alerted me to a contest called the Social Entrepreneur of the Year. He nudged me to participate. At that time, I had no idea what a social entrepreneur was but he said I should qualify.

Many social entrepreneurs participated in the contest. The Swiss and Singapore judges visited each of the contestants, and the finalists included a pastor who created businesses and jobs for former drug offenders; an entrepreneur who employed people with disabilities; and myself promoting sanitation and hygiene.

During the interview, I was asked why our annual expenditure budget was so low at only SGD 2,000, when I was able to host these World Toilet Summits all over the world. I told them the secret of my leverage model is operating at zero cost, since all the costs were paid by the host directly to the event management companies, and the media engagements cost me nothing. I paid only for my own flight and accommodation, which I did not claim since WTO had no money. Hence, the

SGD 2,000 was needed because auditors in Singapore were not allowed by law to do a pro bono audit, so I budgeted this for audit fees.

I was told that the contest was both at contestants' level and in the judging room. During the final selection, the Singaporean judges were against giving me the award because 'Toilets' were not prestigious enough to deserve such an honour to represent Singapore at the World Economic Forum. The Swiss CEO of the Schwab Foundation, Miss Pamela Hartigan, convinced them that World Economic Forum was looking for change-makers who could defy the status quo and break barriers in social innovation rather than merely looking good. I won the contest and became Singapore's first Schwab Fellow of the World Economic Forum in 2006.

I am deeply appreciative of the opportunity for the Toilet and Sanitation Agenda to receive such legitimacy and affirmation and the endorsements from the founders of the World Economic Forum, Mrs Hilde Schwab and Mr Klaus Schwab. I also met the other signatories of the award: writer Paulo Coelho; musician Quincy Jones; Nobel Peace Prize winner Muhammad Yunus; First Lady of South Africa, Zanele Mbeki; and Singapore journalist Han Fook Kwang. They continue to support me and attend other WEF's events around the world every year, which gives me access to the forum's network at the highest echelon of world leaders in corporations, governments, academia and social leaders.

When I met the other social entrepreneurs during my first meeting in Zurich, I felt like a kindergarten kid among adults. I suffered imposter syndrome, feeling unqualified and incompetent to be in the same room as giants in the sector. For example, there was a very humble old man named

Sir Fazle Abed who founded BRAC, which serves 35 per cent of the 100 million people in Bangladesh. There was also Bunker Roy, who taught uneducated grandmothers in India to become solar engineers; Sheela Patel, who helped millions in the slums of India; Thulasiraj Ravilla of the Aravind Eye Care System, which provides free eye care services to the poor, including cataract operations. My mentor Mechai Viravaidya was also there. Everyone was operating with millions of dollars in annual budget except me—alone and without any employees. After two days of interaction, I started thinking how wonderful it would be if all these people were government leaders of ruling countries instead of being social entrepreneurs.

The day after the social entrepreneurs meeting, on the train up the Swiss Alps to the Davos World Economic Forum, I was full of anticipation to meet the highest leaders of the world. I imagined meeting the smartest, wisest, and most powerful leaders, but it wasn't the ideal world I'd imagined.

I noticed that many of the political leaders were reading prepared scripts when delivering their speeches. Although their speeches sounded good, many were not knowledgeable enough to answer unscripted questions from the floor during panel discussions. One of these ministers on stage was from Singapore. She was searching for her notes and was unable to answer questions spontaneously.

I also noticed that the big multinational corporations were there trying to corner markets, but they were not very interested in public good. Many were greenwashing instead of caring about social or environmental issues. The UN folk seemed to be talking round and round without actionable plans. While capitalism is an important driver of growth for nations, the rules of capitalism favour the elite and exclude the interests of the poor. The rich countries are impoverishing the poor countries, extracting their minerals and natural resources, whilst paying them unfairly low prices. For example, Côte d'Ivoire is the world's largest producer of cocoa and the second largest is Ghana. Together they produced more than 50 per cent of the world's cocoa. Yet, the cocoa farmers are extremely poor and Swiss chocolate companies are extremely rich. If the rich can invest in local processing plants inside poor countries, they could transfer skills, create value addition, and slowly bring the poor out of poverty. But they wouldn't do that because weak countries have no negotiating power and are given bad deals.

To be fair, the World Economic Forum is a neutral meeting place to connect people and resources efficiently. The actions of the participants come from their own interests. There are good sides of Davos too. The World Economic Forum has the highest convening power, much like the UN, but is more vibrant. World leaders come to one place to attend a series of important meetings with other leaders, within a few days. This efficiency attracts leaders of all sectors. There were meetings with good outcomes too. For example, climate change awareness was amplified at Davos and that made the world take this issue more seriously. It is necessary that there be such a place for world leaders to meet and reconcile their differences instead of fighting.

The WEF founder, Professor Klaus Schwab, also brought in many communities to balance these behemoth powers of governments and big corporations. They include the Schwab Fellows, Young Global Leaders, Global Shapers, Tech Pioneers, New Champions, the UN leaders, academia, civil society, philanthropists, and the Global Future Council. They also published useful reports and even established an interactive digital platform called Toplink to share knowledge and networks. I also found many leaders who are genuinely passionate about the forum's mission: improving the state of the world. While my idealism was somewhat thwarted, my maturity accelerated. I learned how to live in an imperfect world while keeping my core values intact. I still did not want to grow up. But I now understand grown-ups better. Perhaps, my naïve expectations were due to my limited exposure to the real world. I started thinking about how we can end poverty globally through social entrepreneurship.

Lessons:

A world that operates on greed and charity cannot sustainably end poverty. Donating money to help the poor one by one will not move the needle in a world where there are 4 billion poor. We need system change solutions in order to change the world at scale. Social business is the opportunity where social innovations can balance between profits and purpose and design new solutions, empowering the poor to help themselves. Singapore is a model of development integrating business with social policy.

Delegates at World Toilet Summit 2005

World Toilet Summit 2005:
Terrorist and Toilets

Our member from the UK, Richard Chisnell and Raymond Martin from the British Toilet Association wanted to host the World Toilet Summit 2005 in London, but they were unable to raise the funds needed. Then we read in the newspaper that President Clinton had successfully brokered and funded the peace process in Northern Ireland, and the Irish Republican Army had agreed to denounce terror and dissolve itself. This presented an unprecedented opportunity to utilize the considerable energy and goodwill generated from the peace process to propose collaboration. We negotiated with the Lord Mayor of Belfast to host the World Toilet Summit 2005 in Belfast on 25 September 2005. This was the same historic day when the Irish Republican Army announced the end of its armed campaign and committed to the complete decommissioning of all its weapons.

The World Toilet Summit was funded by the Clinton administration's International Fund for Ireland to demonstrate that Belfast was now safe for international travellers as evidenced by the international conference with visitors from twenty-two countries. This unique fundraising effort shows the gumption of our team to seize the opportunity to establish a relation between terrorism and toilets by creating a narrative to justify funding.

I was also given a tour of the backstreets of London by the Westminster City Council officials. I was appalled to discover that public urination and open defaecation were rampant in a modern city like London. It happens after the pubs close, when there are no public toilets available.

Toilet challenges affect all countries in different ways. That is why we cannot take it for granted. The UK government had been closing public toilets due to lack of budget.[10] It was very disappointing that the UK had so much money to fund wars abroad, but no money to maintain public toilets in their own country.

Raymond Martin said: 'I think germs can kill us faster than wars. We are not being smart about germs and about sanitation. Germs can multiply and mutate so fast and yet the standard of most of these "away from home" toilets is pretty poor. We need to focus on hygiene.'

Lesson:

It is possible to align unlikely alliances if you think laterally. In this case, linking a disarmament of a former terrorist group with the opening of an international event to signify the arrival of a peaceful city allowed us to mobilize money from the Irish International Fund paid by the Clinton administration.

Visit to Star City's Space Station MIR during the
World Toilet Summit 2006

The Second Toilet Coup: World Toilet Summit 2006

Our member the Russian Toilet Association wanted Russia to host the World Toilet Summit 2006 in Moscow. They found a former Soviet Union's KGB Committee of State Security official who could help us connect to the office of the mayor of Moscow. It did not matter that the guy was from the highly feared former secret police of the Soviet Union. In my humanitarian work, I take an inclusive approach. As long as he supported the improvement of sanitation for the Russian people, he was our ally.

I remember what my friend Tony Meloto from the Philippines once taught me: 'If a politician is 90 per cent corrupt, use the last 10 per cent of goodness in him.' Therefore, so long as I was not part of any corrupt practices, I could work on projects with anyone.

The World Toilet Summit 2006 was hosted by Mayor Luzhkov of Moscow, widely seen as the second most powerful man in Russia at that time. He generously allowed us to use the State Duma or the Moscow Parliament House as the venue.

After an unsuccessful attempt to hijack our World Toilet Summit in 2002 and an absence of four years, our member, the Chair of the Korean Clean Toilet Association requested to speak for twenty minutes at our 2006 summit in Moscow. He was then a Congressman in South Korea. I thought that since the 2002 event went well and amicably, we were friends again. Little did I know that a second coup was being planned—the submitted speech was switched and an announcement was made that USD 3.5 million was being given by the Korean government to set up the new General Assembly of the World Toilet Association. It was declared that in 2007, the UN Secretary-General will be the South Korean Mr Ban Ki-moon. Looking at the way WTA was renamed as the General Assembly of the WTA, I imagine the member wanted to boost his status inside Korea in a similar way.

A video was played showing this member as the leader of the General Assembly of the World Toilet Association. Many members of the WTO were already named in the video as endorsing this new endeavour, although they were seeing this video for the first time.

All our delegates were promised that whoever attended the inauguration would be flown on business class tickets with all hotel expenses paid, plus a two-day holiday in Seoul after that meeting. It was further added that unfortunately, Jack Sim had no money to provide for such things.

Instead of winning support, our delegates felt disgusted at the unethical actions to try to hijack our World Toilet Organization for a second time. They also demanded the removal of their names from the video since they never endorsed this new rival.

The member left the summit immediately after being openly reprimanded by several members.

Only two members joined him later, namely from Nigeria and South Africa. They told me later that they'd never flown business class before and explained that this was only a holiday trip for them.

In Moscow, we were treated to a visit to Star City, a restricted exhibition of a replica of the Space Station Mir, and shown how the cosmonauts use the toilets in space, both in their suits and in the station. We learned how urine is recycled into drinking water in space.

Over the next two years, the inauguration event of the General Assembly of the World Toilet Association was promoted through Korean embassies all over the world to invite dignitaries. I stayed calm and did not respond to media questions about the relationship between WTO and WTA.

I was determined not to merit him with any response, because I did not want to lend him my voice. I remember my mother's teaching that it is better not to bad-mouth competitors. I conserved energy to focus on my mission.

By serendipity, a few years later, I met the chairman of The Presidential Council on Nation Branding at a dinner in Seoul after delivering a keynote speech at the World Knowledge Forum. He apologized on behalf of his countryman's behaviour. He assured me it'll not happen again.

Lesson:

The nonprofit industrial complex is competitive. Stay true to your mission and do not be distracted by others.

Indian President A.P.J Abdul Kalam, Dr Bindeshwar Pathak, and Jon Lane, Head of the Water and Sanitation Collaborative Council, at World Toilet Summit 2007

Keynote speech by the Prince of Orange of the Netherlands at World Toilet Summit 2007

World Toilet Summit 2007:
President and Prince

Our WTO member for India, Dr Bindeshwar Pathak, founder of Sulabh International Social Service Organisation, was a man who dedicated his life to building a nationwide sanitation movement in India. His contribution made a difference in the lives of millions of severely disadvantaged poor who couldn't afford toilets. His efforts for over five decades also improved the lives of those who worked as manual scavengers or 'shit cleaners', who are considered Dalits or the untouchable lower caste people of India. He was conferred with the Padma Bhushan in 1991 for social work, the third-highest honour for a civilian.

At first, he was shy to contact me after he cancelled the 2003 World Toilet Summit due to SARS. But I wanted to reconnect with this great humanitarian, so when I heard that his son, Kumar Dilip, was getting married, I asked to be invited to the wedding. Dr Pathak was very happy that I attended the wedding in Delhi, and we became very close friends thereafter.

We worked hard together to bring the World Toilet Summit to India to be the biggest summit yet.

Dr Bindeshwar Pathak hosted our World Toilet Summit 2007, and our guests of honour were Dr A.P.J. Abdul Kalam, the then President of India, and Willem-Alexander, the Prince of Orange of the Netherlands. Their presence elevated the status of sanitation and also increased global respect for the WTO. The Prince has great interest in water management issues and was also the chairman of the Secretary-General of the United Nations' Advisory Board on Water and Sanitation from 2006–2013.

The Prince was a warm and friendly person and a champion for water and sanitation. During our conversation, he asked me: 'Jack, where are all your people?' I replied: 'I am all the people. I have not employed any staff yet.' He was shocked and also impressed that I could build a global sanitation movement alone. He knew I was working with very frugal resources and wanted to help. He became a good friend and supporter, helping us grow awareness of our WTO movement at the UN Secretary-General's Advisory Board for Water and Sanitation where he was the chairman. Both our missions were so aligned and he loved our gumption for championing the neglected Sanitation Agenda so much that he came back as our guest of honour again in 2008 at our World Toilet Summit in Macau, China. This time he also brought his wife, Princess Maxima, who was also a great philanthropist, for social impact. They are both now King and Queen of the Netherlands.

The media coverage of the World Toilet Summit 2007 in India triggered plenty of voices from activists, politicians, and academics, driving massive demand for toilets from the public. Suddenly, the politicians saw toilets as an election agenda and opportunity for popularity. As politicians competed to promise more toilets for the people, our work in India became more prominent. Union Minister Jairam Ramesh became the Toilet Champion promoting sanitation all over India with his Nirmal Bharat Abhiyan or Spotless India Mission.

As the awareness of the importance of sanitation started to spread, this inevitably drove greater demand for toilets. Dr Pathak became inundated with requests to expand his toilet construction efforts and Sulabh International's business grew by leaps and bounds after the World Toilet Summit in 2007. Bollywood movie stars like Vidya Balan became the spokesperson for the sanitation campaigns in many advertisements. The momentum snowballed as more and more people talked about the importance of sanitation.

Dr Pathak was very happy with the legacy left by our summit, and we continued to work very closely together for improving sanitation in India, until he passed away in 2023. He was the embodiment of the spirit of our Sanitation Movement.

His legacy lives on through his son, Kumar Dilip, who is now the president of Sulabh, and we continue to work together for sanitation in India.

Lesson:

Internal resources are always limited. External resources are unlimited.

Leverage external resources through partnerships if you can find the alignments.

The Magical Power of Clean Body and Mind

When Singapore became independent in 1965, we were a very poor country. Countries in Asia were all vying for investments from western countries to create jobs and improve our quality of life.

Our competitors were cities like Hong Kong, Jakarta, Bangkok, and Kuala Lumpur and we needed an extra X factor to win. Our then Prime Minister, Lee Kuan Yew, used the 'power of clean' to end our poverty. He started to sweep the streets with local residents. Clean streets generated a cleanliness culture that attracted foreigners to live here. He introduced a fine of SGD 500 for anyone caught littering, and created an anti-littering habit in the whole country. We also planted trees and flowers and branded ourselves as a clean and green garden city, which turned out to be very profitable. Mr Lee knew that the managing directors and board members of multinational companies needed their wives to be happy before they would decide to relocate to a new city. When their wives fell in love with our trees and flowers, they nudged their husbands to pick Singapore and, in this way, Singapore attracted lots of investments. This, in turn, created jobs and skills training and lifted our people out of poverty. Cleanliness and greenery were visible reminders of the Singapore government's ability to focus, get things done, and deliver results.

Ever since I was young, I have looked up to Lee Kuan Yew's gumption in everything that he did for the country. He understood that if a nation has too many sick people, it will not be productive. To that end, Singapore focused on clean water to prevent water-borne diseases. We cleaned up the Singapore River in ten years, and eventually built a barrage and converted our rivers into reservoirs.

Clean sanitation prevents diseases and produces a healthy and productive workforce. It also saves personal medical costs and the government's healthcare expenditure. Clean toilets are critical for attracting tourism income. Starting from the airport, we impressed our visitors with the provision of 30,000 free-to-use public toilets. We say that airport toilets are the first impression and also the last impression tourists have of Singapore, so it was critical that our toilets be clean at all times.

While physical cleanliness addressed the biological pathogens, the miraculous extension of mental cleanliness allowed us to clean up our secret societies and triad criminal gangs, which are basically pathogens of our society.

In fact, we were able to transform these gangsters into the construction workforce, which helped us build our public housing for the people at affordable prices. Bad people became good people when they came clean. All they wanted was a decent livelihood and care for their families. By doing so, Singapore did not have major drug crises like many other countries. To prevent unemployed youths and youth delinquency, Singapore created vocational schools and polytechnics for those who were less inclined academically. These multiple pathways to success ensured that we could have a low unemployment rate, somewhere between 2 and 3 per cent in any typical year.

The cleanliness mindset also created the expectation of a clean government, and we virtually eliminated corruption within the civil service as a culture in Singapore. We raised the wages of all public servants so there was no need to hustle for 'side income' or under the table money. Today, Singapore's cabinet ministers are paid one of the highest wages in the world.

An ordinary citizen can live his entire life without having to bribe anyone. When the occasional corruption case happens, the entire population reacts in shock and horror, whereas in other countries this may be commonplace. In 1986, Minister of National Development Teh Cheang Wan was investigated for two corruption cases involving about SGD 500,000. The minister committed suicide leaving a suicide note that read: 'I feel responsible for the occurrence of this unfortunate incident and I feel I should accept full responsibility. As an honourable oriental gentleman, I feel it is only right that I should pay the highest penalty for my mistake.'[11] Such cases are very rare because everyone abides by the rule of law in Singapore.

As for our mental health, we also need a clean spirit and soul. There is still a major need to address our stressful and competitive society.

We need to seek calmness and detachment to reduce materialism.

In 2024, Singapore was one of the wealthiest nations measured on a per capita basis[12] in the world, and was able to attract foreign talents and money to invest and work in our country.

We have to stay clean to maintain our quality of life and good cleanliness culture.

Lesson:

Cleanliness starts inside our minds. When we are spiritually clean, we demand clean streets, clean toilets, clean government, clean rivers, and clean air. These in turn deliver safe streets, efficiency, health, productivity, and a high quality of life.

Speaking at the UN General Assembly to all countries' members

The Making of the UN World Toilet Day

During our inaugural World Toilet Summit on 19 November 2001, I declared that day as the World Toilet Day and all the delegates endorsed it. Since then, I have been dreaming of making World Toilet Day a day officially recognized by the UN. I started by sending out open press releases every year about the state of sanitation. I'd suggested campaigns like 'Ten Things to Do on World Toilet Day, 19 November', and these would include sharing the current state of sanitation conditions, how to clean a public toilet, holding a local press conference, creating local activist groups, writing letters to their local politicians, making social media promote World Toilet Day, etc. Surprisingly, the global media continues to give major publicity to World Toilet Day every 19th of November and many international organizations like UNICEF and WaterAid have started using it for their campaigns.

I began to notice that people were now taking up their own initiatives beyond our suggested actions. One novel action taken by an NGO was the creation of the World Toilet Cup during the 2010 FIFA World Cup (using the same acronym

WC) in South Africa. Schools worldwide started using World Toilet Day to teach children handwashing and hygiene; people everywhere were leveraging this auspicious day to speak up and raise their pent-up complaints about sanitation issues. In fact, all UN agencies started to adopt World Toilet Day for their global advocacy programmes. Every year in November, I would become fully booked with global media interviews coming from all corners of the globe.

The media coverage grew with each World Toilet Summit, which often happens on the 19th of November. As the summit was held in a different city each year, the awareness and momentum soon snowballed, garnering bigger and wider media coverage. President Ellen Johnson Sirleaf went 'live' on Liberia's National TV on World Toilet Day to speak about the importance of sanitation.[13] Matt Damon did a publicity stunt with a mock interview about World Toilet Day. World Toilet Day comes alive every year as more and more stakeholders use the day to promote sanitation in their local context. The Germans gave a press conference at Potsdamer Platz in Berlin while sitting on toilet bowls. In Peru, a second-hand toilet marketplace popped up. In Bangalore, there were street protests by women demanding toilets for their houses, while politicians promised to build them if they won the next election. Soon, World Toilet Day began to have very powerful influence on policies and politics and became a very sought after platform by governments everywhere.

Despite all this media attention, I still could not convince any country to table this for deliberation since only member countries could raise such resolutions. Ironically, the opportunity finally came when Mr George Yeo, Singapore's Foreign Affairs Minister, lost the election in 2011. I invited him to be the guest of honour for our World Toilet Summit 2011 in Hainan province to witness the scale of our influence in China.

With Minister George Yeo at the World Toilet Summit 2011

When he arrived in Haikou city, he was pleasantly surprised to see 1,000 Chinese and international officials and experts attending the summit.

He asked me how I did this without resources. I told him that each year, the host for the World Toilet Summit would pay for the cost of the event and also pay WTO USD 50,000 for the hosting rights to host the event. The hosts would also pay for our air tickets and accommodation. I told him we organized the World Toilet Summit every year on a similar scale.

Every country and city has sanitation challenges, and they welcomed the opportunity to leverage our massive media coverage to galvanize their people into action.

After meeting with the Secretary of the Hainan Provincial Party Committee and Hainan's Governor, George asked me if there was anything he could help me with. I requested him to arrange a meeting with our Ministry of Foreign Affairs to discuss the tabling of the UN World Toilet Day resolution at the UN General Assembly.

He immediately called Deputy Secretary Vanu Gopala Menon for help. Menon told George that he could not bring such an embarrassing agenda to the UN. George requested him to give me thirty minutes, and if Menon was still not convinced, he could say no after the meeting. Menon agreed to meet. The meeting lasted ninety minutes as Menon was amazed by our ability to influence so many countries to act on the Sanitation Agenda. He said he never knew this before and agreed to support our proposed resolution.

We flew to meet our UN Permanent Representative of Singapore, Albert Chua, in New York in 2012. Albert arranged for us to make a pitch to the other ambassadors from the Forum of Small States. However, when we arrived, we found out that Albert had been promoted to Second Permanent Secretary, and now had no time to help us. He was too busy preparing to handover his duties to his incoming successor, Karen Tan. According to protocol, we had to wait for Karen Tan to work on the resolution. This could mean a one-year delay, and I was concerned that we might lose momentum if other matters superseded this effort within the next twelve months.

Then, a miracle happened. The ambassadors from the Forum of Small States arrived to listen to my pitch for them to support my resolution. As I began to speak, they bought in and endorsed my proposal, and they told Albert to expedite this. These ambassadors convinced Albert to start, and he agreed. I looked across the table at Menon and saw him smiling.

The next miracle was a surprise. I was told by a senior staff that Permanent Secretary Bilahari Kausikan wanted to use this resolution as an opportunity to train his ambassadors on how to negotiate international treaties. He gave them a target of bringing back at least 100 countries' sponsorships before we tabled the resolution at the UN General Assembly. Every Singapore embassy and foreign high commission worldwide was activated.

To speed up the drafting of the UN resolution, I invited my friend Kenzo Hiroki, a Japanese veteran UN diplomat, to brief our Singapore officers about the intricacies of navigating the UN system for such an effort. Kenzo drafted the UN resolution to designate 2008 as the UN International Year of Sanitation under Prime Minister Hashimoto's leadership, and his experience helped us align all the stakeholders' interests. These included the UN country voting members and the agencies who could not vote but were highly influential.

I made two more trips to New York, staying at the cheapest hotels in Queens. I had to pay for my own expenses, but it was all worth it. We gained early support from most of the members of the Forum of Small States and from all members of the European Union. Then we met China and the USA individually and both agreed to lend their support. Monaco's Ambassador expressed some concern because 19 November is their National Day. But when I reminded him that Monaco's Prince Albert is a Water Champion, he readily agreed to support us.

Then I met the Russian Ambassador who insisted that I change the word 'Toilet' and also the date because 19 November is already a Russian holiday (Day of Missile Forces and Artillery). I told him that it was not possible to change either the name or the date because this had already gained worldwide popularity over the last thirteen years. He said, in that case, he would not support us. I told him, in that case, I would have to tell the global media that the Russian Ambassador did not support sanitation! There was about thirty seconds of tense silence; I did not know what he was thinking. But suddenly, he changed his tone and said that he would support us. I shook his hand and thanked him vigorously. I had no choice but to take that risk.

I thought the Indian meeting would be the easiest since we had been doing so much good work in India. But the Indian

Ambassador told me that he could not support us despite India having the biggest sanitation crisis in the world. The 19th of November was Indira Gandhi's birthday and their National Integration Day, also known as 'Quami Ekta Divas'. I felt his hands were tied, and thought that even without India's vote, we'd have enough to pass the resolution. Meanwhile, all the Singapore embassies collectively exceeded their target with the signatures of 122 sponsoring countries backing our resolution. One hundred and twenty-two votes out of 193 meant an assured win, unless there was an objection or debate. Our ambassadors really made a great effort.

I met Mr Vuk Jeremić of Serbia, who was the president of the UN General Assembly that year. His role at the UN was similar to that of a country's speaker of parliament. He told us that our effort was important and agreed to table our resolution.

On the day of the resolution, our WTO team was awake from 3 a.m. Singapore time watching UN Web TV 'Live' (Singapore is twelve hours ahead of New York time). The UN resolution titled 'Sanitation for All' (A/RES/67/291) for declaring 19 November as the UN World Toilet Day was adopted on 24 July 2013, urging UN member states and relevant stakeholders to encourage behavioural change and implementation of policies to increase access to sanitation among the poor, along with a call to end open-air defaecation. The adoption was unanimous for all 193 countries, and India did not make any objection.

It took us thirteen years to reach this day, and it took less than five minutes to read and approve. They were the longest five minutes of my life.

We were jubilant and called each other in the middle of the night shouting 'The UN World Toilet Day resolution is official now!'

I remember thinking to myself: *If I die tomorrow, at least I would have created a lasting UN legacy for the sanitation movement to accelerate globally.*

Thereafter, Mr Jan Eliasson, the UN Deputy Secretary-General, became our flag bearer, promoting the UN World Toilet Day. He said:

[Sanitation] is an investment. By having sanitation, you can save so much on health and productivity. People go to work. Children go to school. Politicians lack long-term planning. They look at budgetary needs now but don't see the larger picture. But they must look beyond their mandate periods. Ministers of finance should have responsibility for the long-term effects of public expenditure. Water and sanitation cannot drop off the agenda now. There is such a commitment to it. You have the development community, the World Bank, and the big development banks, but also the scientific and health communities along with civil society, and philanthropists all backing it.[14]

The Official UN World Toilet Day Poster

He received the WTO Hall of Fame Award in 2019. Both UN Secretary-Generals, Mr Ban Ki-moon and Mr António Guterres, also gave high visibility speeches for the UN World Toilet Day every year giving the Sanitation Agenda strong legitimacy. Getting World Toilet Day legitimized by the UN was a major win for sanitation globally. I was happy, I was relieved—the taboo of sanitation was slowly being chipped away in every country now.

The UN General Assembly for UN World Toilet Day, 19 Nov 2013

Lesson:

It might take years to happen, but your persistence will get you there.

Getting Bollywood into the Toilet

Speaking at India Today Conclave 2014

I was invited to India Today Conclave 2014, an annual gathering of the elite corporate leaders, political leaders, and celebrities, organized by *India Today*, a major newspaper company. I was speaking as a panellist in a session called 'Salvation vs Sanitation: Toilets before Temples'.[15] BJP leader Uma Bharti and Union Minister Jairam Ramesh were arguing about prioritizing Toilets or Temples. Madhya Pradesh Chief Minister Shivraj Singh Chouhan and I were trying to find the middle ground. They played my three-minute video called 'Meet Mr Toilet' and we finally harmonized everyone's aspirations to get religious leaders to promote sanitation as spirituality since cleanliness is godliness. They were happy to find common ground and agreed to Make Toilet Sexy.

Later, when Bollywood megastar Salman Khan came for his session, I arranged with the host to allow me to ask a question: 'Salman Khan, you are known as the sexiest Bollywood actor. Can you make a film to make toilets sexy?' He was clueless and asked the host who I am. The host introduced me as Mr Toilet. Salman Khan invited me on stage. Upon realizing that I was a Singaporean helping Indians to get toilets, he offered to fundraise for the World Toilet Organization on the spot. He personally donated USD 20,000 and immediately six other companies pledged USD 20,000 each 'live' on national TV that night. It was impromptu, but we raised USD 140,000 that night and all donors were captured 'live' on national TV.

The next morning, I was at Delhi airport. The customs officer recognized my face and asked me if I was with Salman Khan last night on TV? I said, 'Yes.' Suddenly, instead of stamping my passport, he shouted to all the other colleagues to take a photo with me. It was the first time I'd been treated so nicely by custom officers. The power of Bollywood is amazing. A few years later, Bollywood actor Akshay Kumar made a blockbuster movie called *Toilet: A Love Story*.

Salman Khan fundraising for WTO

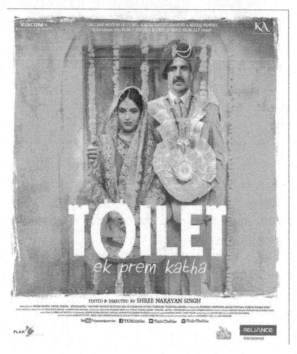

Toilet: A Love Story Movie Poster

With Sarika Saluja and Bollywood megastar Akshay Kumar of the
blockbuster *Toilet: A Love Story*

Lessons:

Be bold and make big requests. If you don't ask, there is
no chance.

If you ask, you either get or don't get, but at least you
have a chance.

Seize the moment when opportunity appears. Celebrities
add the icing to the cake.

Transforming India's Sanitation

After a landslide victory in the 2014 election for his BJP party, Prime Minister Narendra Modi launched the Clean India Mission or Swachh Bharat Mission, a countrywide campaign to achieve an 'Open Defaecation Free' (ODF) India by 2 October 2019 through the construction of public toilets. The objective of the first phase of the mission included eradication of manual scavenging, generating awareness of sanitation best practices, and bringing about a change in the mindset and behaviour regarding hygienic defaecation.

I received a call from Anuraag Saxena, an Indian policy expert living in Singapore. He heard that PM Modi intended to launch a large-scale sanitation revolution for all of India. He believed PM Modi would appreciate the help of the World Toilet Organization. I was excited to work with this lead. He arranged for me to meet Minister of Urban Development Venkaiah Naidu, who became our guest of honour for the World Toilet Summit 2015. This summit was a culmination of our momentum for sanitation improvements in India since our last summit in 2007 with the Indian President Abdul Kalam and the Prince of Orange Willem-Alexander. The WTO's message on the importance of sanitation has been welcomed by the Congress Party, the BJP, and also all the other parties in Southern India.

Because the BJP policies adhere to Hindutva, a Hindu nationalist ideology, we also invited all the religious leaders so that we could mobilize them to become our champions for sanitation in cities and village temples all over India. WTO even joined forces with the prominent H.H. Pujya Swami Chidanand Sarawatiji to start the first World Toilet College in his Parmarth Niketan Ashram in Rishikesh, and we also participated with him in Ujjain's Kumbh Mela 2016 to promote the Swachh Bharat (Clean India) Mission to over 75 million devotees attending the one-month festival.

Around 80 per cent of India's 1.4 billion people are Hindus.[16] Our alignment with Chidanand Sarawatiji was a great partnership for impact as he connected us with politicians and religious leaders all over India. During the fight for independence in 1947, Gandhi was famously known to have said: 'Sanitation is more important than political independence.' This target date of 2 October 2019 for an Open Defaecation Free India, marked the 150th birth anniversary of Mahatma Gandhi and was a brilliant political masterstroke by PM Modi. Traditionally, the image of Gandhi had been associated with the Congress Party since it was controlled by Indira Gandhi's family (who coincidentally had no blood relationship with Mahatma Gandhi). By building toilets nationwide as a present for Gandhi's 150th birthday and using the image of Gandhi's spectacles for the entire campaign, Modi was able to transfer the brand image of Gandhi from the Congress Party to his BJP Party.

To boost PM Modi's speed towards his 2019 target, we worked with the then Hon'ble Chief Minister of Maharashtra,

Shri Devendra Fadnavis, to host the World Toilet Summit 2018 in Mumbai, India's business and entertainment capital, gathering corporations and Bollywood megastar Akshay Kumar to encourage companies to invest 2 per cent of their profits as their corporate social responsibility in the Clean India Mission.

I was invited by many states to work with local governments, activists, and media. These states included Delhi, Gujarat, Haryana, Maharashtra, Uttar Pradesh, Telangana, Andhra Pradesh, Rajasthan, Bihar, Tamil Naidu, Goa, Karnataka, Odisha, West Bengal, and Uttarakhand. On these journeys, I shared with them knowledge, technology, and funding solutions for a very wide range of toilet situations, including railway stations, schools, cities' public toilets, remote tribal villages, city slums, religious buildings, government offices, hospitals, and also lots of different types of places with open defaecation. I was welcomed everywhere, and I've probably travelled to more states than most Indians. I've learned how to cross busy roads, but I don't think I'll ever learn how to drive the way they do. Experiencing their wide range of food, cultures, architecture, and history are some of the rewards for working in India. I know that I'd never have the chance to see all these places if I didn't do social work. I'm richer in experiences this way.

Modi's Toilet Strategy proved unstoppable as it helped Modi win yet another landslide election victory in 2019. PM Modi is a genius politician who aligned the sanitation mission with his political agenda, while actually delivering health, decency, and dignity to his country of 1.4 billion people. In fact, toilets are the competitive edge of any nation because a nation of sick people can never compete on productivity.

The World Toilet Organization is very proud to be one of the partners in this historic project. An estimated 110 million toilets were built during the Swachh Bharat Clean India

Mission Campaign from 2014 to 2019.[17] It was the biggest toilet construction project in the history of mankind. WTO has been active in India since 2007 and work is continuing. For example, in honour of World Toilet Day 2016, Global Citizen gave 80,000 free tickets to a Coldplay concert in Mumbai. In a way, our toilet diplomacy helped Singapore grow a softer humanitarian image beyond the image of a successful business nation. When PM Modi came to Singapore in 2018, we took a two flags photo showing his appreciation of our help to improve sanitation for so many years in India. I hope to do similar toilet diplomacy for Singapore to fly our flag in many more countries.

An official two flags handshake with PM Modi in appreciation of our support for his Swachh Bharat Mission

19 November 2016, Coldplay Concert in Mumbai for
which 80,000 free tickets were given away in conjunction
with World Toilet Day

Lessons:

As a new political party becomes the ruling party, new policies
may emerge as opportunities for major transformations to
take place. Stay alert and have lots of friends looking out for
potential opportunities on your behalf.

Don't forget to leverage on the influence of religious leaders
where appropriate. Do your research to see how to engage
religious leaders effectively, without controversy.

World Toilet College

In 2005, I saw the need for toilet cleaners to be professionally trained. Cleaning public toilets requires much more knowledge, equipment, and skills than cleaning toilets at home. I wanted to start a World Toilet College in Singapore. We had no money, no school licence, no classrooms, and no curriculum. But as always, I started with the needs, worked on the vision of what success looks like, and then worked backwards to plan what resources and processes were needed to achieve the vision.

I applied for the Workforce Development and Job Redesign Grant and received SGD 80,000 to bring professional cleaning experts from Japan to develop the local curriculum and train our master trainers the finesse of public toilet cleaning as well as the cleaners' attitudes and pride. We trained the cleaners in the history of toilets and how hygiene protects us from diseases. After the training, the cleaners realized how meaningful their work was. We video-recorded everything and now have a curriculum. I partnered with the Singapore Polytechnic to use their classrooms on weekends and in the evenings after the students left. I went to the media to publicize the World Toilet

College and soon we had lots of trainees. Their training fees were also substantially subsidized by the government.

The World Toilet College even went international. When Minister of Urban Development Venkaiah Naidu of India agreed to host the World Toilet Summit 2015, H.H. Pujya Swami Chidanand Sarawatiji was very enthusiastic to mobilize religious leaders to support our work. The World Toilet College was launched in Rishikesh, India, in 2016 in partnership with the local partner Global Interfaith Wash Alliance (GIWA) led by Swamiji with support from Miss Patty O'Hayer and Ravi Bhatnagar of Reckitt Benckiser, one of the largest FMCG companies. The college is aimed at driving behaviour change and improving sanitation facilities within the entire sanitation value chain. Through this, we have successfully piloted needs-driven training programmes in the state of Uttarakhand and have trained 5,000 people in sanitation courses.

After the initial success at Rishikesh, World Toilet College expanded its licence further to Aurangabad, Maharashtra, in partnership with Reckitt, Jagran Pehel, and the Maharashtra government, and created the Harpic World Toilet College (HWTC).

Our Courses Include: Toilet Building 101, Sanitation Ambassador Training, Community-Led Total Sanitation, Student-Led Total Sanitation, Professional WINS (WASH in Schools) Training, Capacity Development for Community Workers, Healthy Homes and Families, and Professional Restroom and Toilet Cleaning and Maintenance.

We initially aimed at providing access to modern sanitation facilities and employment opportunities for women through mason training. However, the college saw a perilous job called 'manual scavengers' in maintaining India's outdated sewage system. These sewer divers have to immerse their whole body into the manhole to remove chokage and emerge to dive in again. They breathe in stinking toxic gases and are given a sip of alcohol at intervals. These workers have an average lifespan of only forty years due to constant inhaling of toxic gases.[18] It is a very inhumane job.

The Harpic World Toilet College trained and equipped these workers with machines to clear the choke while standing above ground. The key objective was to improve the quality of life of manual scavengers through their rehabilitation by linking them with dignified livelihood options.

Bhatnagar's holistic approach to the problem was remarkable. He initiated medical treatment for the workers, followed by psychiatric counselling to address their self-esteem and psychological issues. By 2023, the Harpic World Toilet College, in collaboration with non-profit organizations, successfully trained 30,000 sanitation workers—all from diverse backgrounds, varying in age, education, income, and gender— and placed 90 per cent of them into sustainable employment at hospitals, office buildings, and shopping malls.

Now HWTC is also present in Pune, Punjab, Uttarakhand, Kerala, Tamil Nadu, Karnataka, Telangana, Pondicherry, Odisha, Himachal Pradesh, Haryana, Rajasthan, Bihar, Uttar Pradesh, and other parts of Maharashtra. Local partners were brought on board to oversee on-ground implementation, with HWTC serving as the programme's overarching facilitator. The programme translated digital training modules into six languages, launched a compendium containing 101 inspirational stories, and established a referral model within its alumni network to mobilize more sanitation workers.

An independent Social Return on Investment study[19] conducted on HWTC revealed that HWTC's investment of USD 108,000 led to a total social value creation of USD 22 million, showcasing an impressive social return on investment of 1:23. This highlights the substantial positive changes brought about in the lives of sanitation workers and underscores the significance of the programme.

Famous veteran actor Amitabh Bachchan also gave us a donation of twenty-four desludging machines and a septic tank 'Honey Sucker' truck, so that the sewer divers could work on the ground instead of immersing themselves into the manhole. The programme has successfully promoted a sense of self-respect and communal dignity while improving the lives of sanitation workers. We believe it will continue to prolong the longevity of the workers as they do not have to inhale toxic sewage gases while working.

I am very glad to be working in partnership with Reckitt Benckiser and Ravi Bhatnagar and his teams. One of the rewards of doing social work is I get to meet passionate people doing good and work together with them. There is now a major trend of corporations doing good while doing well through ESG. ESG means using Environmental, Social, and Governance factors to assess the sustainability of companies and countries. By embracing ESG, companies increase the morale and pride of their internal workforce knowing that they are working for a socially and environmentally responsible company. Customers are more attracted to companies with such good practices. A high overall sustainability score can also attract investors. I hope to engage more companies like Reckitt Benckiser.

Lesson:

Commercial businesses can partner with non-profit organizations to create a big impact to become responsible corporate citizens. The Corporate Social Responsibility (CSR) trends in the 1990s have now evolved into a compulsory function in many companies to employ a Chief Sustainability Officer to ensure their companies are compliant to stock market guidelines and societal/environmental well-being.

Find the corporate person with a deep passion and support them.

Unsolicited Support

There is a famous quote in the book *The Alchemist* by Paulo Coelho. It says: 'When you really want something, the whole universe conspires in helping you to achieve it.' Here are some instances when WTO's platform was promoted without prior solicitation from me.

Case #1: While filming a movie in Africa, Matt Damon saw that families in a Zambian village lacked access to water and toilets. He realized that you cannot solve poverty without solving water and sanitation. He founded H20 Africa Foundation to raise awareness about safe water on the continent. However, his heavy filming schedule made it difficult to spend an enormous amount of time on his foundation. So, he was delighted when a water engineer named Gary White invited him to be co-founder of Water.org in 2008. Water.org established WaterEquity, investing in water and sanitation enterprises, including microfinance institutions scaling small loans for water and sanitation.

In 2013, Damon created a mock-interview video called 'Strike with Me', promoting the World Toilet Day, 19 November.[20]

Through humour, celebrities, and social media, Damon hoped to raise awareness and inspire people to make a difference. The video reached 1.5 million downloads and increased awareness of World Toilet Day in the USA.

Case #2: The UN issued World Toilet Day stamps on 19 November 2020 to commemorate the twentieth anniversary of the World Toilet Day in denominations of USD 58 cents, 1 Swiss Franc, and 1 Euro. It gave added prominence to the World Toilet Organization and the importance of the Sanitation Agenda at the UN.

Case #3: Out of the blue, I received an email from All Nippon Airways (ANA) asking me if I would accept their air tickets' sponsorship under their Blue Wings programme. They were featuring five Ashoka Fellows for their passengers to donate their miles to. This allowed me free tickets for the next seven years.

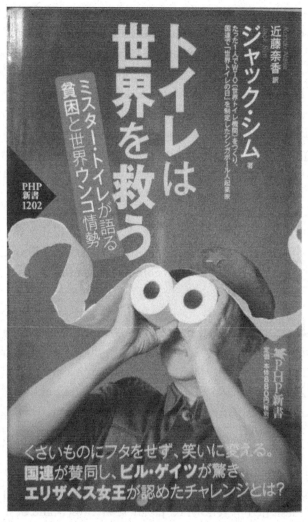

My exploits written in a book called *Toilet Saves the World* in Japanese

Case #4: I was invited by Cartier to speak at their Women Entrepreneurship Conference in Tokyo. After delivering my speech, my host introduced me to the editor of the publishing house PHP Institute, who immediately wanted me to write my story in Japanese. I told them I can only read and write in English. She told me I can speak in English and she can get a translator to help, and after that she can edit it into a book.

They did much research on my stories and previewed media coverage from the internet and sent me a long list of questions. I flew to Tokyo for a full-day interview, and they made a first draft. Thereafter, I flew back to Tokyo for a second full-day interview and sent a series of photographs and that's how the book *Toilet Saves the World* was edited and published in 2019. I went back on a third trip for the book launch and was impressed to see the book available in all the major bookstores like Kinokuniya, Maruzen Nihombashi, Tsutaya, etc. We sold 20,000 copies. I was amused that I was named the author.

Case #5: Cartier created an exhibition of our WTO story at their Dubai World Expo 2020's Women Pavilion, which attracted over 250,000 visitors. They put up the same exhibition during COP28 Women and Gender Pavilion in 2023. They plan to continue this initiative in Osaka, for the World Expo in 2025.

Case #6: Nippon Foundation read my biography published by PHP Institute and contacted me to help promote their Tokyo Toilet Project featuring seventeen amazing public toilets designed by renowned Japanese architects and designers. They paid the WTO USD 70,000 for our consultancy and also convinced the Ministry of Transport to approve a budget of USD 250,000 to host our World Toilet Summit 2021 in Tokyo. Our plan was to invite government officials from all over the world to come and learn how the Japanese managed to have the cleanest toilets in the world. We planned to make Japanese Toilet Culture the next big export of Japan, similar to Japanese food, J-Pop, cosplay, and manga, just to name a few.

Due to Covid-19, the Olympic Games Tokyo 2020 were postponed to July 2021. However, the events were largely held with no public spectators permitted due to the pandemic. Unfortunately, our World Toilet Summit 2021 was cancelled as there was no end of the pandemic in sight.

Case #7: When I met Muhammed Ishaq Amin, a Nigerian student, at the Lee Kuan Yew School of Public Policy, I asked him if he knew the Minister of Water Resources of Nigeria. He made the introduction and within a month, Nigeria announced that they will host the World Toilet Summit 2022 in Abuja and it'll be opened by the Nigerian President Muhammadu Buhari and UN Deputy Secretary-General Miss Amina Mohammed. The Nigerian World Toilet Summit was attended by all thirty-six states' governors and it led to a comprehensive blueprint to end open defaecation for all of Nigeria by 2025 as a target.

World Toilet Summit 2022 in Abuja, Nigeria

With Samoa's Prime Minister Tuila'epa Sa'ilele Malielegaoi

With Fatima Strickland in local traditional dressing

Case #8: Samoa Honorary Title

After the UN declared 19 November as the UN World Toilet Day in 2013, I received a phone call from Mr Tuilaepa Sailele Malielegaoi, the Prime Minister of Samoa. He invited me to Samoa to receive an honorary title as the Chieftain in one of his villages. I asked him why he was giving me such an honour when I didn't do anything for Samoa. He told me, the name of the village Falevao means Toilet Village, the only village in the world called 'Toilet Village'. Since I am the Chief of Toilets of the world, I should be Chief of Toilet Village in Samoa. I accepted the honour.

Julie and I flew to Samoa via New Zealand. I was inducted at dawn in a Religious Kava Ceremony with the other village elders of Falevao Village. We drank from the same pot of sacred Kava juice and I became one of them with the Matai title of 'Tuifalevao' meaning High Chief of Falevao Village.

Others who also received such a matai title were All Blacks coach Steve Hansen, who is also a three-time World Rugby Coach of the Year; former New Zealand Prime Minister John Key; Robert Muldoon; and UN Secretary-General Ban Ki-moon. I hope to meet fellow Samoans like Dwayne Johnson, Keenu Reeves, or Jason Momoa one day.

Lesson:

Life is a series of unforeseeable events. Go with the flow, don't resist the flow. And it'll take you to unexpected places.

Opening of the World Toilet Summit 2019 in
Sao Paulo, Brazil

Lobbying the Senate at Brasília 2019

Some years ago, a business delegation from Brazil visited Singapore and I was one of the speakers at that conference. The Head of the Globosat and TV Globo group was inspired by our work and invited me to speak at Globo's annual event. I met them at their Rio de Janeiro event and since they owned all the main TV stations in Brazil, they asked me to stay for several TV shows to talk about toilets. They also introduced me to Trata Brasil, an NGO lobbying for waste water treatment. Fifty per cent of all the human waste discharged in Brazil was untreated and this polluted their rivers and beaches. That was equivalent to 5,300 Olympic-size swimming pools of untreated sewage dumped into nature daily. The negative costs on health, loss of income, loss of clean drinking water, and loss of tourism income were astronomical. Yet, 94 per cent of the wastewater treatment plants in Brazil were state-owned and they had no money to invest nor the capacity and efficiency to manage hi-tech plants. We decided to rally for support for a World Toilet Summit 2019 in Sao Paulo on 19 November, World Toilet Day, to gather all stakeholders to solve this challenge.

One key piece of the solution was to lobby the Brazilian Senate to pass a Private-Public-Partnership bill allowing private investments into government-owned sewage treatment plants, and improving the management of these plants to make them profitable. The trade unions were against it because they feared that privatization might lead to job losses due to efficiency. Together with Trata Brasil, I lobbied seventy-nine senators in September 2019 at the capital, Brasília. I told them that the 100 million Brazilians living in favelas (slums) are waiting to vote for them in the next election, when they are happy with their new sewage connection provided. I told them that the union's objection will not gain popular support, and they have nothing to worry about.

They knew I had the support of media giants like Globosat, TV Globo, and other news channels that would create massive media coverage accredited to them. They were convinced and the bill for the 'New Legal Framework for Basic Sanitation' was passed with sixty-five voting in our favour and thirteen voting against it with one abstention. My passionate plea was translated from English to Portuguese and it worked. I have to thank the simultaneous translation crew for an equally passionate translation. The bill was then processed and Brazil's president, Jair Bolsonaro, signed the new sanitation bill into law on 9 July 2020 after congress approved a new regulatory framework for the sanitation sector to facilitate increased participation by private sector firms.[21]

Since the approval, eighteen contracts comprising PPPs and concessions were signed with total investments worth around 68 billion reais (USD 14 billion).[22]

The government hopes to attract up to 700 billion reais (around USD 134 billion) of private investment towards its goal of universal access to sanitation services by 2033.

I was back in Sao Paulo in 2023 and visited a favela where the sewage connections were done. It was really heart-warming to see the actual life improvement of the local people and the pride they had now that their houses were connected to sewage treatment. The stink in the village is now gone and incidents of related diseases are also reducing.

Lessons:

Step into the shoes of the people you are trying to motivate, and understand how they might feel.

Design narratives that can incentivize them into action.

Once you feel it in your gut that the majority of your audience will agree with you, go with the pitch, and take the chance.

You do not need all the people to agree, as long as there is enough per cent to get to 'yes'.

How to Create an Award

Each year, the World Toilet Organization Hall of Fame Award recognizes outstanding efforts of governments, academia, corporations, multilateral agencies, and activists for their dedication in improving sanitation conditions globally. The award work in many miraculous ways:

1. It honours and gives recognition to the exemplary work of the awardee.
2. It helps raise the status of the Sanitation Agenda every year.
3. The amazing work of the awardees inspire others to do the same.
4. The media coverage generates mass awareness and visibility of the importance of sanitation.
5. The awardees continue to be our ambassadors to grow the impact of sanitation globally.
6. These awards remind us that although Sanitation is an underdog agenda, there is no shortage of champions in our sector.

7. The World Toilet Organization's role is to convene, orchestrate, and energize these champions and all stakeholders to become champions for sanitation.

8. When an eminent person accepts the award, he or she is also endorsing the award and giving equity to the others in an inclusive manner.

Our laureates include the former UN Deputy Secretary-General Jan Eliasson who championed the Water and Sanitation Agenda inside the UN; Nigerian Minister of Water Resources Suleiman Hussein Adamu who made Nigeria the African nation with the biggest sanitation investments; Rose George, author of *The Big Necessity: The Unmentionable World of Human Waste and Why It Matters*, which brought toilet awareness globally; UN Deputy Secretary-General Aminah Mohd; Ravi Bhatnagar of Reckitt; Dr Bindeshwar Pathak; and Trata Brasil who raised about USD 12 billion investments for Brazilian Wastewater and Sewage Treatment Plants in Brazil.

Lessons:

1. Awards are beneficial for both the awarder and the awardee. Consider the kinds of awards you may create that align with your mission.

2. The higher the eminence of the awardees, the higher the legitimacy they bring to the mission.

3. Awards recognize, motivate, amplify the importance of your agenda and encourage new stakeholders to come forward to support your mission.

4. Be inclusive with awardees across all continents, genders, and nationalities.

Time Magazine Hero
of the Environment 2008

When I gave an interview to Hannah Beech, *Time* Magazine's Head of East Asia, I thought it was a deep dive into the impact created by the World Toilet Organization.[23] I told her how the poor had prioritized having a cell phone instead of having a toilet, and how I have to sell the importance of hygiene and sanitation to governments and politicians to move the needle. We discussed how poop and pee can become fertilizers and biogas for cooking, and such recycling is helpful in mitigating the effects of climate change, and how we should protect our rivers from sewage pollution. I even told her how I convinced the Singapore government to change the building codes to provide for more ladies' cubicles so that they do not have to queue for public toilets. It was a very long interview.

My role as a storyteller is to serve every journalist like they're my benefactors. A week after the interview, she sent me for a professional photoshoot. Little did I know she would name me a *Time* Magazine's Heroes of The Environment 2008. Furthermore, I received this accolade together with actor Arnold

Schwarzenegger, advertising moguls Jean-François Decaux and
Jean-Charles Decaux, Peter Head of Arup, and others. Having
my name on the front cover of *Time* Magazine was a big
surprise. I must admit that I suffered a mild bout of imposter's
syndrome the day I read the publication. I bought ten physical
copies of the magazine to keep in mint condition. I told myself,
enjoy it a little but use it to help the people without sanitation.

Since I started WTO, I've been interviewed by thousands
of media outlets. At first, I felt exhilarated. I felt famous and
my ego was boosted. Then, I started to feel that something
was not right. I started this mission to do good and not to be
famous. If I continued to become intoxicated by fame, I might
soon become narcissistic. I reminded myself that my mission
is paramount, and the mission is not about me. I saw many
well-meaning peers trapped inside a fame-craving mode.

I speak to myself and understand that the purpose of media
visibility is to create legitimacy for the mission and it is good to
keep amplifying the mission. I'm a storyteller and the story is
about the people's need for safely managed sanitation.

So how do I reconcile with this insuperable pride that keeps
popping up?

I learned that the ego cannot be killed, my ego is a tool
I must manage well and use for the greater good. The trick
is to be aware of the ego and to come to terms with it as a
healthy working partner. First, I had to remind myself daily,
and as I matured, I was better able to manage my emotions
in order to shorten the 'ego' enjoyment to a minimum, so that
the mission remained paramount and higher than myself.
I must say humility takes lots of practice, and I don't always
succeed. But I know it is working when my speeches are not
about myself, but about the mission. I know it when more and
more people take ownership of the mission and act in their own

right. The more people take action, the more it becomes their mission and then, the mission assumes a life of its own. The more I lose control, the wider it grows, just like nature's fractals repeating the patterns virally. Instead of being a hero, my role is to make others champions for the mission and to do it in their own names without the need to acknowledge us.

Lessons:

You are not the mission.

Your mission is higher than you.

Fame is intoxicating, media visibility is for strengthening the legitimacy of the mission and not for your personal fame.

People will not support you if they think you are doing it for your own glory.

Always remember your mission. Manage your ego.

Fundraising photo with President Clinton

Clinton Global Initiative

The Clinton Global Initiative (CGI) was founded by President Clinton to address big challenges, create new opportunities, and make a difference in people's lives around the world. When I was invited in 2008 to make a commitment with President Clinton in Hong Kong, I thought this might be a big breakthrough for sanitation funding. Fundraising with President Clinton turned out to be rather simple: You queue up with about ten specially selected CGI Fellows, and take the photo with the President, then you go and fundraise yourself. After that, you report back to CGI annually on how much money was raised using that photo. I thought CGI would introduce me to lots of potential donors, but that was not how it works. I have to find my own donors.

After taking that photo, President Clinton gave me an idea: he told me that since the highest hand in poker is the royal flush, I should contact ESPN's World Series of Poker to do a fundraising round where they might agree to play to raise funds for the WTO. However, CGI did not introduce me to

ESPN nor to any donors since they were also fundraising for themselves in order to keep the CGI operating.

Interestingly, although it looks like optics, the legitimacy of the photo helped elevate our charisma level and we raised USD 1.2 million for WTO. A major portion of the funds raised came from the Singapore Economic Development Board, which was then starting an International Organization Programme Office and looking for made-in-Singapore international organizations, and other donors also joined in.

I'm still hoping to get the contact of the right person at ESPN's World Series of Poker.

Lessons:

There are many ways of giving.

Some may give you money, others lend you their influence, talent, voice, clout, time, service, expertise, advice, and also give in kind like hardware or software.

Take whatever is useful and use them.

I did not do my social work to win awards. But awards help me do my work better.

Our SaniShop logo

SaniShop: The Power of Jealousy

The concept of SaniShop as an economic empowerment micro-franchise was conceived when I began seeking a more sustainable solution for improving sanitation delivery beyond the traditional charity model, which was unable to solve the scale of the global sanitation challenges. There simply weren't enough donors interested in toilets.

The best way forward was to turn the sanitation crisis into a massive business opportunity that increased the economic viability of the poor so that they could lift themselves out of their poor sanitation conditions. Rather than simply waiting for government action or charitable handouts, I realized that the key was to train the locals, building their capacity by making them entrepreneurs, creating local jobs and income from simple production and sales set-ups.

In 2009, I partnered with the Lien Foundation to establish a new NGO called Lien AID that matched USD 100,000 to a USD 100,000 grant from USAID to set up SaniShop in Kampong Chhnang, Cambodia, a self-sustaining business selling toilets and sanitary equipment to the locals.

I started to talk to the villagers to understand their mindsets about buying a toilet. The women mostly wanted a toilet in their house. But the men who held the decisions were a mixed group. Some worried about money. Some said that since traditionally no one had toilets, why do we need it now? Others said they have bushes in their land to poop, so they do not need toilets, only people without land need toilets. I observed that there were many types of poor and how they spent their money on snacks, cigarettes, alcohol, gambling, religious offerings, and festivals like New Year, Gods' birthdays, harvest time feast, coming-of-age ceremonies, and curing diseases. Toilets were not a priority in their financial expenditures.

I introduced SaniShop to motivate all stakeholders including the local governments and communities to create an efficient market for toilets. To drive supply, we mobilized the masonry shops and transferred some simple technology to produce simple twin-pit toilets casted with concrete using locally welded metal moulds. To drive demand, we selected local traditional village gossipmongers (the equivalent of today's 'online influencers') to be our salesforce. These gossipmongers instigated jealousy among the homeowners by making the toilet a status symbol of success.

The motivation to own a toilet leveraged on the idea that everyone wanted to keep up with the Joneses, and hence triggered an emotionally driven change in behaviour, making toilets a desirable product. Immediately, the first early adopters prioritized toilets in their financial plans. To make the toilets affordable, we created a tontine system where six to eight families would pool their funds every month to buy one toilet costing about USD 100. Each month, they'd draw lots to see who won that toilet of the month, and the families continued to pool their funds until all families had toilets. In this way, they did not have to borrow high-interest loans from the loan sharks. After the first 20 per cent of early adopters built their toilets, the rest wanted to follow. We learned that the human nature of jealousy and shame are the same regardless of wealth or status, and we applied the same marketing strategy of selling a Louis Vuitton handbag in Paris to the village level and it worked very well.

I remember when our family was poor, the floors of the village houses were either made of cement or mud. Those families with cement floors would look down on those with mud floors, and when the mud-floor families could afford their cement floors, they usually paid a bit more to add colours making it a red cement floor. This was their way of fighting back as if to say, 'I am wealthier than you.' When we moved to the government housing HDB flat, there was a similar 'floor war' when neighbours upgraded to terrazzo floor, ceramic tiles, and even marble floorings just to show off their status. As we grew into middle-income, everyone started competing on the size and brands of their cars.

SaniShop became a successful self-help micro-franchise in Cambodia in 2010. We built 20,000 household latrines just in Cambodia and trained over 570 sales entrepreneurs. iDE Cambodia simultaneously improved on the same model with funding from the Bill & Melinda Gates Foundation, the Stone Family Foundation, the World Bank GWSP, and the Global Sanitation Fund, and rapidly scaled up sanitation marketing and reached 30 per cent rural sanitation coverage by 2015. During the project period, iDE facilitated the sale of more than 141,096 improved latrines to rural households reaching 663,151 people.[24] In 2019, they raised a USD 10 million Development Impact Bond to develop rural sanitation markets in six Cambodian provinces. iDE Cambodia was awarded the

WTO Hall of Fame Award for this phenomenal success. The model was eventually adopted by the Cambodian Ministry of Rural Development as a national programme.

Lessons:

Remember that your users are people too. They have emotions, desires, and fears. These emotions can be useful if we deploy them strategically.

Drive the demand first, and the solutions for supply become market-driven.

Create and prove a solution and then give it to others who can scale it up better than you can. You cannot do everything yourself if you want to solve huge problems.

Women's Equal Right to Toilets

Why is it that ladies often have to queue up for public toilets whereas the gents' toilets seldom have queues? Women claim that it is normal for them to queue to pee, but I think this needs to change.

There was a design flaw by the architects who always designed equal spaces for the male and female toilets. This space allocation has been a historical inequity for more than a century. Before the women's liberation movement from the 1960s to 1980s, women did not have the freedom to go out of their house as much as men. Few women were working in the past and when they did go out, they were usually accompanied by their father, brother, or husband. This meant that the need for ladies' toilet allocation was sufficient at that time, if one provided equal spaces to both gender toilets.

However, as both men and women began to work and travel, the demand for toilets equalized. Women were disadvantaged as the gents have many urinals that take up less space than a cubicle. Studies by YouGov have shown that women need about ninety seconds to pee, whereas men need forty seconds.

Fifty-nine per cent women said they have to queue often but only 11 per cent of men said the same.[25]

Women have to close the door, hang their handbag, inspect the toilet seat cover, undress, and then pee. If they happen to be menstruating, they may need time to change their sanitary pad. They also need more time to wash their hands (which men may sometimes forget to do) and more mirror time to do their make-up. In contrast, men only need forty seconds to pee as they have to unzip, pee, and zip. This resulted in long queues in the ladies' toilets and no queue in the gents'.

I approached AWARE (Association of Women Action and Research), the leading women's rights and gender equality group in Singapore, to join forces to tackle this problem. They rejected my proposal as trivial and unworthy of their participation. They told me they were more focused on family violence and other more important matters rather than talking about toilets. In the end, I did not get their support and I had to push equal toilet rights for women myself.

It took ten months to draft the proposal for a new Code of Practice for Public Health with our National Environment Agency and inter-agency consultations before it became law. Since 2005, all new non-residential buildings have to allocate much bigger space when building ladies' toilets to accommodate more cubicles. This has shortened or eliminated the queues for ladies in all new buildings completed after 2007. This same law has now also been adopted in China and other countries.

Ironically, the fight for women's rights for bigger toilet space was advocated by a man, when the women's advocacy group refused to take up the challenge. It is a reminder that although gendered lack of access to toilet facilities may be a daily inconvenience and injustice, discussing toilets is still somehow felt to be out of bounds for polite and serious people.

I hope this building code can become a universal standard in all countries one day. Perhaps female activists all over the world can take up this challenge in their respective communities and jurisdictions to lobby for the local building codes to accommodate this change. I'd be very happy to help any of them if the readers here can connect me to them. We should promote Potty Parity worldwide.

Lesson:

The world was designed for men. Now we need to help redesign it for men, women, and all genders—including when it comes to toilets.

World Toilet Day's Poo Pee Happy Sculpture at
Marina Barrage, Singapore

Poo Pee Happy

After our founding day 19 November became the official UN World Toilet Day, I requested the Public Utilities Board (PUB) to allow me to build a monument in Singapore commemorating this historic event. Afterall, this was the first time that Singapore had single-handedly tabled a UN resolution and successfully managed to get the resolution adopted unanimously by all 193 countries at the UN General Assembly. I wanted Singaporeans today and future generations to be proud of this. The PUB donated a small piece of land at the entrance to the Marina Barrage, a well-visited site.

Meanwhile, Dave Holland, an accomplished advertising professional, told me he had been following the WTO progress and felt we needed to update WTO's branding image from my original amateurish designs, and he offered to do it for free. In the new branding, Dave added three icons that captured our mission. The three human action figures in the 'Poo Pee and Happy' mascot are self-explanatory, the humour in this branding aligns with WTO's cheeky style of communication. I was very happy with his designs.

I decided to use these three icons for the UN World Toilet Day's monument. I've never built a monument before, so I asked around and narrowed it down to a reliable vendor who quoted SGD 30,000 for a coloured stainless steel ten feet structure with a black-marble base.

I approached a real estate developer, Mr Tan Soo Sam, to fund the erection of the monument. I told him the prime land allocated to us by the government for free was worth more than the cost of the sculpture; and that the monument he built would forever commemorate our country's first UN resolution at the UN General Assembly. His name will also be inscribed there forever. He generously donated SGD 30,000 and the sculpture was made in Taiwan and shipped to Singapore.

In fundraising, when trying to persuade donors, it is important to go to the heart of what they care about most. As a real estate developer, Mr Tan appreciated the fact that the land given free by the government was something very rare. And as a Singaporean, he felt proud to be involved with an initiative that commemorated Singapore's achievement in the declaration of the UN World Toilet Day. Both these aspects touched his heart in the right place, catalysing his generous action.

Lesson:

Imagine an idea. Imagine the resources and actors you need to achieve the idea. Assemble these resources and actors to create an outcome.

Sell the idea to each of them in ways that would motivate them.

Imagine people will say 'yes' to your requests and ask for help.

If the first one was a 'no', keep asking others until you get to a 'yes'.

Gates Foundation Reinventing the Toilet

The Bill & Melinda Gates Foundation is primarily focused on health. But they realized that almost half the world's population has no choice but to use unsafe sanitation facilities, resulting in half a million children under age five perishing every year from diseases like typhoid, diarrhoea, and cholera. A total USD 223 billion in health costs and productivity losses. Bringing safe, affordable sanitation to the world would also act as a 'super-vaccine' that would effectively end the spread of many deadly diseases.

Bill and Melinda Gates realized that prevention is cheaper than cure and they initiated the Reinvent the Toilet Challenge to spur the creation of new toilet technologies that safely and effectively manage human waste.

The initiative has resulted in more than twenty-five breakthrough technologies that are available for commercialization by product and sanitation service companies.

Donors know that WTO is the voice of sanitation globally, but before they agree to fund us, they want to know what was the measurable deliverable impact of WTO's work.

Although I know that WTO is popular, I've never had money to measure our impact or how many people we've reached. That's why we remain frugal because we don't know how to make promises to the donors. Some outcomes take years to materialize and we have to keep working on them through a journey of obstacles.

In 2011, I was overjoyed to be invited by the Gates Foundation to apply for a grant to support WTO's advocacy work. Having no experience in fundraising, I asked for USD 200,000 wondering if it is too much to ask for. I flew to Seattle and was told that I should add another USD 70,000 for a consultant to measure our advocacy outreach. They gave me a total of USD 270,000. I was so happy and jumping with joy for getting such a huge grant.

Later, a peer told me I'd asked for too little. He asked for USD 2 million and got it. I felt naïve but I'd learned my lesson. When you're new to something, don't be complacent in your ignorance and do as much research as you can. In the grant application, I promised to promote sanitation awareness with a target to reach 100 million people. We paid USD 70,000 to Meltwater media monitoring and their analysis report revealed that World Toilet Organization and World Toilet Day had reached 2.1 billion people across online news, social media, print, broadcast, and podcasts that year! This was an outstanding accomplishment, beyond what I had ever dreamed possible. Sanitation advocacy has become a belief system with a life of its own and it is spreading fast.

We continue to work with the Gates Foundation's Reinvented Toilet programme. We sit on their committee on setting the ISO standards for off-grid sanitation products. They funded many of our World Toilet Summits, policy influence events, and we are now developing an app to calculate the cost of negative externalities to persuade governments to prioritize investing in sanitation. I am glad that Bill Gates is now willing to associate himself with poop. In fact, when I saw him at Beijing's Reinvented Toilet Conference, he was displaying a bottle of poop on the rostrum when delivering his speech. We have another big champion for sanitation!

Lesson:

Before asking for donor's support, always do your research as to how much to ask by checking on how much they've funded others. If you ask for too little, you lose the opportunity to scale up your work. If you ask for too much, they say NO and the conversation might end.

Amplifying Sanitation Opportunities

When I met Neeta Pokhrel, Director of Water and Urban Development at the Asian Development Bank (ADB) in Jakarta, she pulled me aside and told me that governments are not paying enough attention to sanitation and we need to find a way to motivate them to prioritize sanitation. ADB can also provide loans to these governments if they qualify after due diligence. She called me the 'Best Salesman in Sanitation' and said I should think up a solution.

I remember a UN research publication by the famous development economist Guy Hutton, showing every dollar invested in water and sanitation can give a $4.3 return in the form of reduced healthcare costs,[26] loss of productivity, and prevention of mortality. However, Guy's papers are very technical and long. In order to convince time-deficit politicians and senior officers to understand his theories and parameters of measurement in a simplified narrative, I had to develop a digital tool to produce evidence to support decision-making.

I assembled a team headed by Anusuiya Radika Sarmah, an intern from the Lee Kuan Yew School of Public Policy, supported by our General Manager, Sarika Saluja, and a tech team consisting of Pratibimb Dwivedi and Artur Wala. We consulted with Guy Hutton and developed the 'SanOpps' project to convert data into evidence of sanitation opportunities for decision-makers in different cities. The idea was to create a digital tool for evaluating the cost of inadequate sanitation by pricing all its externalities to demonstrate that not having sanitation and hygiene cost more than its investments. With the evidence and data to justify investments in sanitation, I could further customize our proposals according to our intended audience's needs and values.

The Bill & Melinda Gates Foundation approved a small grant for a manual pilot version in 2024 and we will test it in Nagpur and Dehradun in India. Thereafter, we can digitize the model and scale it to multiple cities and countries. It's going to take another two years to test and develop the complete software. When completed, I'll create a training course to train all the activists how to use SanOpps to motivate decision-makers and drive political will to invest in sanitation. In the process, ADB, World Bank, Inter-American Development Bank, Africa Development Bank, and New Development Bank (established by BRICS), can all enjoy this open-source tool and training curriculum to increase their loan portfolio in sanitation loans.

Lesson:

Finding solutions is like a funnel. You start with guessing potential pathways towards the end outcome. These are experiments and not solutions yet.

With each experiment, you engage outside resources to form teams to help refine the answers.

As you continue forward, the picture of the outcomes gets clearer and nearer to you.

Keep refining and improving on the ideas, and it'll become more workable with each iteration.

Poster for my biopic *Mr Toilet: The World's #2 Man*, launched at Hot Docs Canadian International Documentary Festival in Toronto, Canada

Mr Toilet, the World's #2 Man

Jessica Yu, an Oscar-winner for documentary films, was the first person to document my sanitation work, with her excellent three-minute short film called *Meet Mr Toilet*. She has miraculously squeezed a great summary story of Mr Toilet's work within three minutes, covering the taboo of shit, the problems caused by the silence, how I made Toilet Sexy, and the footages of me in Singapore, India, Indonesia, and the USA. She even inserted an animation clip of Mr Toilet in the film. Its opening lines were a shock to the audience. The scene shows me saying: 'When we were children, our parents told us not to talk about shit. This is a serious problem, what you don't talk about, you cannot improve.'[27]

Jessica told me that when it premiered at the Sundance Film Festival in Salt Lake City in 2012, it was received enthusiastically and lots of people wanted to meet Mr Toilet and were asking if he was at the festival. Sadly, I was busy at another event in Saudi Arabia that day. So, when she told me that this short film will be the opening act at the Cannes Lions International Festival of Creativity at Le Palais des Festivals,

Cannes, in 2013, I decided to go with my daughter Faith to give
her some exposure. Cannes Lions was equivalent to the Oscars
of the advertising industry. Every advertising agency dreams of
winning one of those lion-figurine awards. I learned that the
WTO is a welcome candidate for aspiring advertising agencies
to use us as a pro bono client.

In 2013, I received a call from a freelance journalist called
Lily Zepeda who wanted to write an article on the Gates
Foundation's Reinventing the Toilet Project. After our phone
interview, she was so inspired that she decided to quit her job
as a journalist to become a film-maker. She told me that she
finally found the perfect subject for her film. I was extremely
flattered. At the time, I thought she'd probably take three to six
months to shoot the film but I was wrong. The film ended up
taking six years to complete!

There were many reasons it took so long. Lily had to raise
funds to produce the film entirely on her own. She started with a
donation of USD 100,000 from the sanitary ware manufacturer
Kohler. It wasn't enough to make the film. But she was certain
that she would be able to raise more funds. Whenever she ran
out of funds, she'd pause the project and wait for more investors,
sponsors, and donors to appear. It was her journey of gumption.
Nothing was certain but she was sustained by her passion and
delivered a great film to tell this story. At the time, she lived in
her boyfriend's house and saved on rent to stay frugal. She did
some part-time work as well but the film was central to her life.
She worked, slept, and breathed for the film.

Her energy also sustained her production team of three, who
were very supportive. They did not have a story to begin with.
They simply followed me to see how the story would develop
and guided her on potential scenes to shoot. They edited a huge
amount of footage into a story in the sixth year. For whatever

that was missing in the footage, they used animation to bridge the story gaps.

She eventually raised a total of USD 600,000 to complete the film, including a year of editing and pitching for appearance at film festivals worldwide.

To make a documentary with a series of story arcs, she had to wait for dramatic events to happen in my life, and she'd shoot them whenever such events happened. For example, there was an episode where all my board members resigned after we ran out of money and she shot that. There was also a colourful event when we gathered at the Ujjain Kumbh Mela in 2016, a Hindu festival with over 75 million devotees. Our partner was H.H. Pujya Swami Chidanand Saraswatiji who worked with religious leaders to promote sanitation in India.

The film was shot in four countries, namely Singapore, India, China, and the USA. We needed to fit the schedule of the writers and editors Tchavdar Gerogiev, Hee-Jae Park, and Monique Zavistovski, as they all had other films to do. Some of the personalities she persuaded to appear on the film included ESM Goh Chok Tong, the former Prime Minister of Singapore; Singapore's former Foreign Affairs Minister George Yeo; my wife, Julie, and our four kids; the legendary Dr Bindeshwar Pathak of Sulabh International, and others. I was really impressed by her ability to mobilize resources.

Over the years, we got to know each other very well. There were times she ran out of money for the film. Other times I ran out of money too. But we both survived to tell the story.

Lily did not let me preview the film until the opening day at Toronto's Hot Docs Canadian International Documentary Festival 2019. I was very happy that she had produced an honest-to-goodness film. It didn't hide my failures, limitations, and idiosyncrasies. It won the Docs for Schools Award and also the prize for 'Award This! Socially Relevant Documentary'.

Lily Zepeda devoted six years of her life and raised all the funds to make this film possible. I salute her gumption and tenacity. She is truly a model of gumption. She had the perseverance to convert her belief into reality. The film was very well produced. (I'm biased but you can watch it for yourself.[28]) It balances the perspectives from my family members, the politicians, the activists, my staff, my departing board members, and many others. I felt it was an honest depiction of my journey as Mr Toilet and even gave me new insights of my weaknesses. I was also surprised to hear what my children said and how they felt about an absent father that they got used to. Julie even cried during one scene. The film was the product of consistency and hard work. I couldn't be prouder of it.

Lesson:

Gumption is a word that encompasses many other words. Some of them are curiosity, courage, passion, tenacity, creativity, etc. Lily is the embodiment of so many of these words.

It was her first and only film. But she produced a quality that won prizes at film festivals worldwide. Just as Lily was fully immersed in her project, you can achieve success if you persist all the way.

The Future of Toilets in Healthcare

We all know that prevention is better than cure, but doctors can only cure us when we are sick. They cannot prevent us from getting sick.

What if I told you that the toilet may become the game-changer in our healthcare systems?

A 2020 Stanford study reported that a disease-detecting 'precision health' toilet has the ability to analyse urine and stool samples, and then scan for any potential illnesses.[29]

By 2023, such commercial smart toilet products have already appeared at the annual CES technology show. A smart toilet can carry out longitudinal monitoring to detect early stages of cancer and many other diseases, much more accurately than a one-off medical examination.

Our daily downloads of urine and faeces are actually key data for our health if we can capture them efficiently and non-intrusively. With the advancement of technologies in sensors, cameras, nano-nose, genomics, and more, we are able to use our excrement to detect diseases at early stages or predict them even before their onset.[30] The toilet can then offset a major cost of hospitalization once we shift our attention to detection instead of cure. For example, colorectal cancer is a silent killer. If you discover it at the third or fourth stage, the cost of treatment and operation can cost up to USD 500,000, or it may be fatal. However, if it is discovered at stage one or two, it is perfectly and affordably curable. The same benefits will apply to many other diseases, not to mention sparing the whole family from unnecessary anxiety and trauma.

There is already a Poop Bank called AMILI in Singapore that stores healthy poop in deep freeze for retrieval in case a poop transplant is needed in future. Healthy poop is rich in good bacteria and can be extracted when a person is at peak physical health. At a later age, that same poop can be transplanted back into the same donor's gut to treat a myriad of diseases. This works in the same way as the cryopreservation of umbilical cord tissue for babies, which are rich in stem cells. AMILI's Series A has already raised USD 10.5 million.[31]

Beyond the toilet bowl, other facilities inside the bathroom can also augment healthcare diagnostics. Smart mirrors have the potential to detect skin diseases. In the future, a person may have access to various health evaluation services such as spit tests, throat photography, eye tests for glaucoma and cataract, and hearing tests—all within the confines of a high-tech toilet. Toilet paper may even become sampling tools.

With economies of scale, the toilet might one day replace half of all hospitals as diagnostics are done at home in the toilets and reports are immediately sent to the individual's cell phone. This lowering of cost can also democratize healthcare further to reach the poor at the base of the pyramid as well.

Insurance companies may benefit a lot here with lower claims, although pharmaceutical companies may lose some. We have to start promoting predictive and preventive medicine as the default approach to healthcare.

The smart toilet needs heavy investments and long clinical trials in hospitals to verify its efficacy as an FDA (Food and Drug Authority, USA) certified health device. Many products are starting with the consumer market first, where the barriers are lower.

Technology is moving very fast. We might be able to reduce the number of hospital beds by replacing it with the toilet as a diagnostic centre.

Lesson:

The toilet is a data-collecting centre. If data is gold, the toilet data is black gold.

I devised a Theory of Change on how we could incentivise each stakeholder, from public agencies to private entities, to assume ownership of the agenda.

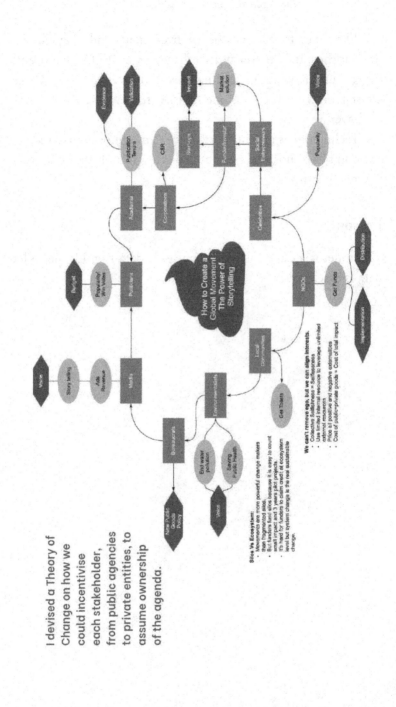

Silos Vs Ecosystem:
- Movements are more powerful change makers than fragmented silos.
- But funders fund silos because it is easy to count small impact and 3 years pilot projects.
- It's hard for funders to claim credit of ecosystem level but system change is the real sustainable change.

We can't remove ego, but we can align interests.
- Collective Selfishness = Selflessness
- Use limited internal resource to leverage unlimited external resources
- Price it (positive and negative externalities)
- Cost of public+private goods = Cost of total impact

The Collective Power of Selfishness

All our lives, we are told to become somebody. We are cultivated to celebrate heroes. We wish to become a hero if we can. However, when we are addressing a massive challenge beyond our own capacity to solve, we should abandon our aspiration to be a hero because we need others to join in the effort. If we are narcissistic about being a hero, others might not join, and our ego becomes the obstacle to our mission. To create a movement, we invite everyone towards a common mission. We have to be inclusive and not exclusive.

That said, there is a place for selfishness. The World Toilet Organization's Theory of Change is founded on collaboration through collective selfishness (the idea that all parties are mainly interested in getting what they want).

1. **Engaging the Media to Drive Awareness and Demand:** The media legitimizes our mission, our messages, and our status reaching billions of audiences with billions of dollars of advertising value. Meanwhile, our unique blend of humour and serious facts shocks

readers and increases the readership, circulation, and advertising income for the media. This symbiotic relationship between WTO and the media is durable and continuous as it is mutually satisfying.

2. **Motivating Political Will:** WTO has effectively raised awareness around the issue of proper toilets among the public, which could potentially earn popularity votes for politicians who align themselves with the cause. This in turn attracts politicians to work with the WTO. The exploitation moves from bilateral to triangular when the politicians make promises of toilets to the people.

3. **Driving Good Policy:** To implement policies well, they need to mobilize their civil servants to plan policies and allocate budgets. These decisions have to be evidence-based, which leads us to academia.

4. **Bringing Evidence:** Governments often consult with the WTO on policy planning. We then bring the academics to support civil servants using cost-benefit-analysis based on their research. In doing so, governments gain expertise to craft strong policies and the academics gain credibility through publication and implementation. In the university culture, if professors don't publish, they perish. So researchers are always thankful for such opportunities to publish and to be referenced.

5. **Engaging International Systems:** The UN can help but they are typically very slow and bureaucratic. To be efficient, we work outside their system and launch with them when we are ready. They like it this way as it speeds up the process, while they bless our common mission with their legitimacy. We are also highly visible at other global platforms like the World Economic Forum, Clinton Global Initiatives, etc.

6. **Making Sanitation Sexy:** Celebrities add the icing on the cake and make the mission sexy, drawing their massive fans and new followers to the mission, while enhancing their image of generosity.

7. **Corporate Partnerships:** The corporations support the mission to fulfil their Corporate Social Responsibility (CSR), Corporate Shared Values (CSV), and Environment Social Governance (ESG) sustainability. Such practices enhance their competitiveness while simultaneously advancing the economic and social conditions in the communities in which it operates. Our partnership with Reckitt on the Harpic World Toilet Colleges is a good example.

8. **Social Business:** Companies like Lixil started for-profit companies producing low-cost sanitation treatment systems with very affordable terms to the poor.[32]

9. **Foreign Direct Assistance:** Foreign Aid agencies provide Official Development Assistance (ODA) fundings to financially invest in the mission. Funding also comes from national, state, and city governments.

10. **Venture Philanthropy:** Philanthropists and donors who are now aware, invest or donate to the cause.[33]

11. **Philanthropists/Donors:** Charity monies can be good for pilots, experimentations, research, and capacity building. This can be blended with other sources of support to kickstart ideas.

12. **Investors:** If a solution can be profitable (e.g. the Brazilian Wastewater case), it can be more scalable to solve the problem commercially.

13. **Implementation:** The NGOs and social entrepreneurs receive the funding and implement their sanitation projects with the people. The people learn to build,

            clean, maintain, and empty the toilets on the ground so
            as to enjoy the facilities sustainably.

14. **Start-ups:** There is now a growing pipeline of start-ups
        designing new systems for delivering sanitation.

15. **Setting Industrial Standards:** The Bill & Melinda
        Gates Foundation invested in technology and also ISO
        standards for Safely Managed Sanitation systems.

The result of this ecosystem is more and more people have access to safely managed sanitation, and other countries adopt similar interventions learning from the successes of others.

As you can see, each stakeholder who joins the ecosystem takes away what they want and yet, their collective selfishness becomes selflessness. This is because we cannot kill the ego. Do not ask people to make their ego smaller. Ask them to make their ego bigger, far bigger than they can possibly achieve. That's when you can motivate them to do collective selfishness (politely known as a win-win).

When you can orchestrate collective selfishness towards a purposeful and meaningful common mission (e.g. to end global poverty, climate change, etc) this collective selfishness can simultaneously produce selflessness.

This ecosystem can grow and grow with a life of its own, as long as we feed the catalysts continuously to orchestrate the trust building across sectors and geographies to generate more mutual exploitations.

The conductor in an orchestra does not play an instrument. He orchestrates each and every musician to perform their best in harmony with all the other players. He listens to each sound produced and calibrates while motivating everyone to embrace a common mission of transmitting a unified vision of the music out to the audience.

In a similar way, my role as the orchestrator of the sanitation movement is to keep all stakeholders motivated in giving priority to improving the state of sanitation. Unlike the orchestra where the conductor is on centre stage, the success of facilitating the sanitation stakeholders is achieved by putting them on centre stage. We cannot compete with our stakeholders in the limelight. They need to take ownership of their part of the work and do it in their own names.

Our global community needs to learn how to become a caring community of parts as well. We move as one cohesive body. This is how we can collectively create a selfless ecosystem in our society.

Our society is like a Swiss watch with all the components disassembled and fragmented. All we need to do is to assemble all the pieces together into a fine piece of machine and everyone will do their part to make a collaborative society.

OUR VISION - TOGETHER THROUGH EFFECTIVE COLLABORATION

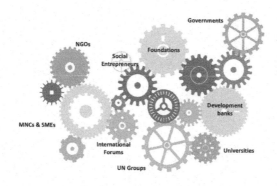

Harmonizing all stakeholders to work efficiently
and effectively like a Swiss watch

Lesson:

Collaboration comes from collective selfishness, which leads to selflessness.

Motivate and Incentivize Others to Get Things Done

Moralizing vs Solving

We often moralize about what is right or wrong, but ranting gets us nowhere. What is more important is to get people to act. Even if they agree with me but don't act, nothing will happen, and I'd have wasted my time in the discourse. Moralizing is merely stating my position without strategy. This may even alienate some people and lead to unnecessary confrontation or loss of goodwill. It is useless to win an argument and miss the mission.

There are several forms of pugilistic arts. Boxing, karate, or taekwondo are confrontational because they rely on violence and inflicting damage. Such actions are against the flow of each other's energies, because they are destructive in a relationship.

On the other hand, judo, aikido, and tai-chi rely on the natural flow of energy, using the force of the opponent instead of one's own.

If you know what motivates a person, you can incentivize him into action in the direction that they are useful in.

There are three levels of motivation.

First, at the organizational level, they want to deliver excellence in their duties, in the interests of their organization within their scope of duty. An officer might want to deliver his key performance indicators but he might also need visibility in his superiors' eyes.

At a personal level, they act according to their individual motivations of likes, personal history, and aspirations. A politician might want to improve the quality of life of his people, but he also wants to be popular, win votes, and stay in power. He needs to appeal to the communities loyal to him as well as attract new supporters.

At societal level, their relationships with their communities may require them to behave in certain ways. The norms should be factored when designing incentives systems to motivate them.

Once you understand your collaborators' motivations, you need to act to influence them.

As you can see throughout this book, I have been doing things I don't know and somehow got many of them done. My key formula is the Leverage Model of External Resources:

1. **Other people's money** (banks, investors, donors, sponsors): There is no such thing as a good business without investors or funders. Make irresistible deals and let the funders chase you for partnership. Don't be afraid to be a minority shareholder and let others manage. Hypothetically, if you are a 20 per cent shareholder in ten companies, that's 200 per cent shareholding with

others working hard to grow the businesses for you. If you have to fully manage one company, you cannot create new ones. If you can borrow the bank's money, you can scale your activities. Stay useful in any partnership.

2. **Other people's talents, time, and expertise** (pro bono services, advisors, volunteers): If you can use other people's staff, there is no need to employ your own. The more staff you own, the more time you'll have to spend talking to them. To pay them, you have to employ fundraising staff, which incurs even more overheads. Many NGOs fall into this trap as they rapidly expand their number of employees and are always running out of money. That model is stressful and inefficient. If you can learn from other people's experiences, you don't have to make lots of mistakes to reach the answers, so their advice is valuable.

3. **Other people's influence** (policy influence, money influence, media influence, etc.): Be respectful, humble, and likeable. Nobody can trust you before they like you. After they like you, they are happy to help you.

4. **Other people's power** (soft powers, hard powers, relationship powers, etc.): Understand the dynamics of power from personality, positions, honour, respect, trust, allegiance, religions, associations, popularity, and obligations. Powers are like strands of string. When you weave them into a network, it produces synergy to give and receive each other's power. If you can, align, facilitate, and orchestrate everyone's power to unlock their collective exponential power.

5. **Other people's assets** (IP, models, technologies, hardware, software, branding, etc.): Donating a digital licence of software costs nothing to the donor, but it's worth a lot to you. Brand associations can be

mutually empowering. There are lots of second-hand machines and hardware in the First World that you can recycle for great value in the developing world.

6. **Other people's dreams** (align the dreams and aspirations of all the stakeholders): Everyone has dreams, if you know what they are, you can help them fulfil their dreams while doing the same for others.

7. **Other people's authority** (UN, government, politicians, academia, religious leaders, corporations, foundations, etc.): The highest impact you can create is policy change and system change. Working on system change may take a long time, but the impact is large and long-term.

I've compiled a mud map of the motivations of all the stakeholders and a rough guide on how to incentivize each of them. If you accompany this with your customized narratives and personal charisma, chances are that you may achieve whatever you dream. Your key take away is, 'You can achieve everything, as long as you can get others to do it.'

STAKEHOLDER INCENTIVES

	Funders/ Donors	Investors	Technologists	Social Entrepreneurs	NGO'S	Local Communities	Government	Politicians	Media
More Revenue Streams		X	X	X	X	X			
Save Time	X	X	X	X	X	X	X	X	X
Save Cost	X	X	X	X	X	X	X	X	X
Co-Design	X	X	X	X	X	X	X	X	
Co-Buy	X	X	X	X	X	X	X	X	
Co-Distribute	X	X	X	X	X	X	X	X	
Get Recognised	X	X	X	X	X	X		X	X
Increase Profit	X	X	X	X	X	X	X	X	
Increase Outreach	X	X	X	X	X	X	X	X	X
Access Knowledge	X	X	X	X	X	X	X	X	X
Database Access	X	X	X	X	X	X	X	X	X
Avoid Mistakes	X	X	X	X	X	X	X	X	X
Learn and implement ideas	X	X	X	X	X	X	X	X	X
Copy+Good	X	X	X	X	X	X	X	X	X
Business Relationship	X	X	X	X	X	X	X	X	X
Social Bonding	X	X	X	X	X	X	X	X	X
Identity and Status					X			X	

Incentives Chart by Jack Sim

Lessons:

If you don't remember anything in this chapter, you just have to remember OP—Other People's . . . and you will remember how to get others to help you. No matter how big your organization, your internal resources are always limited. But your external resources are unlimited. They are yours for the asking. If you have nothing to offer one party in exchange, you can leverage other parties to give them what they need. Your role as an orchestrator assembling all the component assets into a Swiss watch makes you valuable to everyone.

Summary of Milestones, Achievements, and Structures

It is difficult to measure the impact of a global movement because a movement involves all players and the attributions of the resulting impact should be accredited to everyone who has participated. The other difficulty is that the change in impact cannot be measured based on instant gratification or short-term transactions, but the results can be seen over decades.

I've often been asked how I should quantify the role of the WTO in impact measurement. I tell them it is easier to answer that question with another question: What would have happened if no one broke the taboo of sanitation? What would the world look like if the WTO did not exist twenty-four years ago?

Since the founding of the World Toilet movement, it has created an exponential impact:

- **Beneficiaries: 2.5 billion** people have gained access to proper sanitation
- **Awareness: 3 billion** audience reached annually

- **Events: 19 World Toilet Summits** with lasting legacies
- **Toilets Built: 110 million** toilets built in **India**
- **Culture Change: All Tourist Toilets in China are Clean**
- **Capacity Building: 15 Harpic World Toilet Colleges** with 30,000 sanitation workers trained and placed into jobs in India
- **Investments: USD 14 billion** investments in **Brazil Sewage**
- **Africa: 36** states of **Nigeria** towards Open Defecation Free by 2025
- **Legitimacy: Broke taboo** on sanitation with the creation of UN World Toilet Day

One little-known fact is WTO actually achieved all these with a very small and frugal team. In the first seven years, it was a one-man-show with me alone. In our seventh year, we received some funding and employed our first staff. This grew to nine staff but with the end of the grant, we ran out of money. Today, WTO has two full-time staff and one part-time staff. This is the miraculous sustainability of our leverage model of social entrepreneurship.

I have been working for free for the last twenty-seven years, and my family survived on the passive rental income from the properties I invested in at age forty. Some years, we operate on zero dollars. The show must go on, and it can run on an empty tank with will power. I used to write cheques to WTO mostly for staff salaries. These accumulated to hundreds of thousands of dollars. Eventually, I waived all these personal loans. WTO is debt-free and now I have to find talented and passionate people to take over the helm for a WTO 2.0 future. There are still lots of people without toilets, lots of poorly maintained toilets, and lots of improvements we can make for safely managed sanitation to be available for all the people on the planet.

WTO now needs a new kind of leadership, one who can make it a professionally operated global institution that can attract support for this important work.

I will continue to be the storyteller, something that I can do well. I'll assemble the next generation to hand this over to in a few years. There is a time to start, time to grow, time to hand over.

Lessons:

Know your strength, know your weakness. You can run on an empty tank if you can fuel it with passion. But each stage of an organization needs different types of leadership. The mission is higher than the leader.

How to Have a Forever Romance

For more than three decades, I've been busy working and travelling and have not spent much time with Julie. I'm away from Singapore about 30 per cent of the time each year, travelling mostly for my social work. Even for the days I am in Singapore, I am only at home for dinner less than once a week because of work and meetings. It is fortunate that in her vivacious nature, she has made plenty of good friends and support networks that she is never lonely without me. She was happy before she met me. She is happy after she married me. She is a happy and confident person by nature, and that has been the foundation of our happy marriage. She is also very forgiving and accepts me for who I am and does not try to change me. One of the greatest prizes in life is to find the love of your life. I am eternally grateful to Julie for accepting me as her husband. Many friends asked me why I am always praising her in conversations. I told them she smiles at me every day and I am blessed to have such a wife.

After being married to her for about ten years, I asked her why she chose me over the other suitors. She said I make her laugh all the time. I discovered three ingredients for a joyful marriage:

1.   Surprise. Humour. Laughter. Instead of sending her flowers (which are expensive), I'd sketch a caricature of myself with a bouquet of flowers and send it to her office. Her colleagues would pick it up from the fax machine and talk about it. Nowadays, I take pictures of beautiful flowers and WhatsApp them to her. Surprises cannot be regular. They need creative thoughts. She knows I'm frugal and doesn't expect me to buy expensive stuff. But once in a while, I do.

2.   Esteem. Respect is key. Besides telling her I love her daily, I have a habit of telling others about my wonderful wife behind her back. Inevitably, there will be relatives or friends who tell these tales back to her and make her feel appreciated. These revelations also help prevent me from straying, since friends expect me to be faithful after telling them how I appreciate my wife.

3.   Pleasure. One of the biggest gifts was to have domestic helpers to do the cleaning, washing, cooking, and help with the kids when they were young. It's important that she is not overworked. She needs time for leisure and to meet friends.

In 2014, I paid SGD 4,000 for a new hybrid unnamed species of orchid and named it after Julie. The species was named *Julie Guarisophelya* to be registered at the London Registry of Orchids by the local farmer. I didn't do it when he told me later that the registration cost is another USD 4,000. The twelve pots of these beautiful orchids did not flower again after the first bloom, and all we had was the photographs of the flower. It was a foolish waste of money to be thrill-seeking.

Throughout our marriage, we've only quarrelled twice, and both were about my mother's behaviour, not about ourselves. Differences between in-laws are sensitive to handle, but I learned a new skill to resolve such disputes. I told both my mother and Julie separately that I love both of them and should not be a middleman in such disputes. Since I have no problems with either of them, they should deal directly without my participation. Without me as the 'free channel' to vent their frustration, they suppress their frustration and things never explode into quarrels any more, and I've returned to my status as a loving son and loving husband.

I am quite different from Julie. After adulthood, I almost never invested time in friends and rarely spent any time drinking coffee with anyone unless we were working on some mutual projects. I was always driven by objectives and considered aimless chit-chatting a waste of time unless it was an inquisitive process or there were intellectual exchanges. There were times when I sat next to Julie in the car listening to her on long phone calls with her friends over trivialities. She told me that's how you make friends. She was right; I actually have no intimate friends, although I have many good friends. My only intimate friend is Julie.

Our romance started during our first meeting. Julie was sitting in a coffee house in Johor Bahru in a red dress. I'm blessed to live this romantic journey with her every day. The excitement to see her each day makes me wonder why I should be away from her most of the time. As I age, I've grown to be addicted to her more. She's like a battery charger giving me energy whenever we hold hands or hug. I want to retire from all responsibilities in the next five years and travel with her often. She told me she'll believe it when she sees it. She doesn't believe I'd retire into that sea cruise around the world that we've discussed. Let's see what happens. I've started taking short trips with her to the Genting Highlands in Malaysia and Hội An in Vietnam, and I am enjoying it very much.

Lesson:

A happy wife makes a happy life. Make her feel precious all the time, and you'll be rewarded abundantly.

Front Row (Left to Right): Earth, Julie, Jack, Faith

Back Row (Left to Right): Truth, Worth

56

Becoming a Father

Nothing is more fulfilling than having children. Even my career or social work are not as important as my family. In fact, having a family strengthens a man to do his work.

I watched the birth of my firstborn, Faith. As I was in the delivery room looking at this little vulnerable baby next to her mother, I suddenly felt the weight of fatherhood. I cannot fail in this mission until she is independent. This baby needed me and I felt a sense of duty I've never felt before. The next morning, I stopped climbing scaffoldings on construction sites, something that I did often to inspect the installations of my building products. I became risk-averse. I could not die before my mission as a father was accomplished. With each subsequent birth, I concentrated on how to provide for them financially in a stable manner. When I saw others having a baby, I saw a lovely baby, but when it came to myself, the feeling was not intellectual, it was spiritual. Truth came three years later, followed by Worth and Earth in consecutive years.

I gave them names of virtues in the hope that they become good people when they grow up. During the early years of the children's growing years, I spent a lot of time playing with them. But I was often away from home. So, I taught them that their mother is their God. She gave birth to them and they should always respect her and never upset her. In a way, I've effectively outsourced their upbringing to Julie and abdicated a large portion of my duty as a father. I behaved like a person free from the constraints of family. One of the things that helped mitigate the challenges of Julie running the household was the fact that we had two domestic maids to clean up the house and help her care for the kids when they were very young and always running around on their own. When I was around, I remember often losing one of the four kids in shopping centres whenever I was entrusted by Julie to watch over them while she shopped. I'd go to the information counter to report the loss of a child or was getting alerted by the public announcement that a child has been found. Julie often told me that I was her fifth kid the way I behaved.

Many friends and relatives told me I was an irresponsible father. They were not wrong, but Julie told me, 'Don't worry. Just do whatever makes you happy. The most important thing is to be happy.' I feel very blessed and often wonder how my life would have become had it not been for Julie and all her support. I am certain that the World Toilet Organization would not be very successful if I was not a free soul. Beyond time, it was also the freedom to dream up crazy ideas, always knowing that I was fully supported by her.

I learned from the Center of Fathering to give each child a 'personal night-out' each month and I did that for about two years bringing them to movies and game arcades and walks. Eventually, as they grew up, they told me I was boring as I kept trying to give them 'graduation speeches' about life, instead of just playing with them. I wondered why the other kids in universities loved to listen to these speeches but not my kids. They told me those university kids didn't have to listen to the same lessons repeated fifty times. I realized that was the hazard of being my children. I learned that I cannot teach children to be who I am nor who I wish they could be. They needed to figure that out themselves, just like I've figured it out myself.

It is a learning journey, and years later, I often felt I should have done better. You can't go back in time, and nothing prepares you to be a father. Just when you think you know how to handle things, they become teenagers and you have to adjust again.

Under Singapore's education system, co-curricular activities (CCAs) are a core component of the holistic education received by youths. Its purpose is to inculcate values and develop competencies beyond academic studies. All secondary school students are required to take part in at least one CCA, which counts as merits for entry to tertiary education at age sixteen. We planned for Earth to learn the erhu, a Chinese two-string violin, during her primary school. This allowed her to get direct entry into a good secondary school.

I made the mistake of sending Earth to Chung Cheng High School. They were very big on their Chinese Music Orchestra. Earth learned how to play the erhu till the eighth grade. Her school was often in the top three in Chinese Music Orchestra inter-school competition every year. Her team even got to play alongside a pop-star during one of his big concerts in Singapore. Her school's principal was very proud of their achievements. But Earth was not happy. She told me that the long hours of music practice the school demanded were torture as they robbed her of her childhood. After she graduated from Chung Cheng High School, she never touched her erhu, not until today. It was difficult for me to see how much it affected her. Forced learning can take away all the fun from learning. Education should be for the healthy development of the child and not for the glory of the school. That was when I realized that something had to be done for the Singaporean education system.

Each year, we bring our kids overseas at least once to experience different countries, food, and cultures. We've covered all continents from Iceland to Australia, the USA to Japan, China, Eastern and Western Europe, Turkey, Middle East, India, and many others. These travels broadened their exposure and helped them overcome their prejudices and embrace acceptance of otherness. From history to technology, arts, music, performances, religions, architectures, politics, communication, to farms, slums, opulence, poverty, opportunities, and the lack of it. They learned the story of human nature, how our species has lived, loved, fought, killed, obeyed, defied, rebelled, reconciled, and repeated the same confusing behaviours again and again. Although they grew up in the same family, they were very different in character and personalities. They also took away different perspectives from the same exposures. This is why each human is unique, and their influences include their school's environment, friends, media exposures, and personal encounters. We each live inside a unique personal universe and yet we need to harmonize our universe with those of others.

Faith went to Melbourne University and the Singapore Management University. Truth went to Geelong Grammar School in Melbourne and the University of Exeter in the UK. Worth stayed in Singapore and studied in the Nanyang Technological University. Earth went to Singapore Polytechnic and the College of Fashion in London. As they studied in different countries for years, I didn't meet them often.

While Julie would have long regular overseas calls with each of them, I would join these calls only when I happened to be around Julie at that moment. I did not follow their personal development as a father. I thought I only needed to know that they're fine, and Julie would give them the motherly care and support as usual, which she did.

While Covid-19 was a global crisis, it was also the first time that I spent so much quality time with my family, and I was glad to have gotten to know them better during that period. I was also glad that they've grown to become decent and independent people. During this lockdown period, I also learned that it is quite fun to be with them if I stop trying to teach them heavy lessons like I used to before. We played mahjong every day. Through the family bonding, I discovered that I should enjoy time with my kids more because time will not allow us such togetherness once they form their own family nucleus and have kids of their own.

We resumed our family trips after Covid. What they've inherited from us is the education they received and the values Julie and I have inculcated in them as role models. We hope we were able to inspire them as parents. There should be some leftover money when Julie and I pass away, but I believe they're going to be proud that they've succeeded in their respective lives with their own abilities. I told them not to wait for their inheritance because they'd be in their fifties or even sixties when that happens, and if they are unable to stand on their own two feet by that age, they'd be in trouble themselves. They told me not to worry and that they'll be fine. Hearing that, I felt proud.

The joy of fatherhood is derived from your ability to give unconditional love and the magical process of watching them grow into capable independent adults making decisions of their own. Although they are your own, you never actually own them. For the child to grow, parents have to learn to let go. The family is not about ownership. The family is about belonging to a bedrock, which is also the reliable launching pad for each of our personal journeys.

Lessons:

Children make you a responsible person. The joy they bring is priceless.

Do not deprive your children from the struggle to learn the skills of survival so that they'll teach their children and grandchildren how to be independent and proud individuals, and let them step out of your shadow.

The 65,000 sq. ft. SDG Center at 26 Ubi Rd4 Singapore

Covid Crisis and the SDG Center

After age forty, I stopped borrowing money from the bank because the mental stress of my previous financial crisis was a lesson I did not want to repeat. I was comfortable collecting rentals and working as a full-time volunteer for social causes. Then something happened and I was seduced into seizing an opportunity that required me to borrow money again.

The Mass Rapid Transit (MRT) station was built right in front of Besco Building. I convinced my brother we should rebuild our old building into a 60,000 square feet new building (three times the current space). It cost SGD 10 million to build, and we borrowed SGD 8 million from the bank. A series of unfortunate events started to unfold. Our contractor abandoned the site midway through the construction, when his subcontractor was unable to continue due to the financial crisis. We had to re-tender for a new contractor, which increased the cost by another SGD 1.5 million. Our claim against the first contractor incurred SGD 3 million more losses in legal fees. Besco started to suffer business losses due to declining market demand. The building delays added more holding costs with rising interest rates. And when the building was finally completed, Covid-19 came and the building was largely empty for about three years without rental income. In total, we lost about SGD 6 million due to the combination of such factors.

This was the second major loss in our lives but we did not suffer the same emotional anxieties associated with the 1997 financial crisis. You may say that we were now very experienced in losing money and could mentally handle it better. As most of our wealth was tied up in property assets, both William and I had to empty our life savings from the Central Provident Funds. We also emptied our own cash savings and borrowed some money from our wives. He sold one of his shophouses and reduced our bank loan. Within a year, I returned to Besco, restructured the leadership, and the new team made a profit within the next twelve months. There was no panic. We accepted that adversity can happen and some losses are normal, as long as we can continue our normal lifestyles. In a way, money seems unreal when we can lose so much money and yet feel detached from it. We think of the three scenarios: What could be the worst situation? We met our bankers and showed them that our property assets far exceeded the amount we owe them. We told them we'd sell some of these properties but it'll take time to find a buyer. Meanwhile, we will pay interest but not capital repayment. They agreed. Our only focus was how to get the cash flow normal without disruption. I reduced the size of the company, fired our General Manager and promoted three young staff to run the company. The young guys were enthusiastic but they were clueless as to how to run the business. I introduced them to the bankers, simplified the decision process and after about six months of coaching, I let them make decisions autonomously. The first year after they took over, we moved from losses to a small profit. The second year, they made SGD 300,000.

I've been a business partner with William for forty years now. I am very appreciative that we've never quarrelled about money before. We told ourselves that we came from poverty, and to be able to live such a good life is already a blessing.

The building is now almost fully occupied. The Singapore Red Cross Academy is now our tenant, collaborating with the World Toilet Organization and the BoP Hub on designing humanitarian solutions.

Lessons:

Money problems are about money. They're not about emotions. Stay calm because being emotional doesn't solve the money problems, it can only make it worse when you worry. Keep a clear mind and find answers by facing life squarely.

How to Deal with Bureaucrazy

As a Singaporean, I naturally love Singapore. But I couldn't understand why bureaucrats always reject my proposals for improvements. At first, I was angry, but it didn't help. As I defined my relationship with Singapore by the rejections I received from the bureaucrats, the pain of caring for Singapore became unbearable and I wanted to run away from this unrequited love. I decided to give up trying to help Singapore and applied to migrate to Australia. I got our Australian Permanent Residency Visas approved for the whole family. I sent Truth to Geelong Grammar Boarding School and Faith to Trinity College in Melbourne. I started looking to buy a house in Melbourne.

However, I eventually asked myself why should I go and live in other people's country just because my government is not listening to me? I changed my mind and stayed in Singapore.

Despite having business successes, I was continuously seeking knowledge to compensate for my lack of formal education. I always felt inadequate for not having a degree. During a family dinner, my mother mentioned that unlike her siblings, none of her three children are university graduates. I told her I can do it. She laughingly told me I'm too old for that. I wanted to make her proud. Since I was often frustrated by bureaucrats who rejected my ideas, I decided to find out by entering their mindsets. I enrolled for a part-time Master's in Public Policy degree at the Lee Kuan Yew School of Public Policy (LKYSPP) in 2009. I told them I was too old for a Bachelors and applied for a waiver quoting my life experiences. They accepted my pitch.

I studied the ploys of bureaucrats and politicians, and how they work with and against each other. My aha moment in the course came when my Professor Dean William asked me this question: 'Are you frustrated with the bureaucrats, or are you frustrated with your inability to mobilize them?'

I realized that I needed to improve my ability to mobilize them. I empathized with them and focused on how to mobilize them and help them do their work with even higher impact. It's not their fault that they have limited powers and that their powers are often fragmented because solutions to my proposals require multiple agencies and authorities beyond an individual scope of duty.

Through my friendly interviews with many classmates who are bureaucrats, I discovered what I call 'Jack's Law of Bureaucrazy'.

If an innovative idea is submitted to the bureaucrat, here are four of their most common reactions:

Option 1: Reject – This is the default step because it is safe to do nothing. Bureaucrats are incentivized to make no mistakes and are risk-averse. Work avoidance is their default mode.

Option 2: Eject – Send the innovator for the run around to other departments and agencies. Tell him this is not the right department. This is another work avoidance tactic.

Option 3: Deject – If the innovator insists on coming back, leave him hanging in mid-air with non-committal replies. Let him feel the hopelessness of waiting and give up.

Option 4: Hijack – In case the innovator attracts your superiors who like the idea, hijack the idea and claim it as your own.

To make it simple, if I can cut to the chase and make him hijack my ideas immediately, a motivated bureaucrat would create the desired system change at a much faster speed.

Knowing the above Jack's Law of Bureaucrazy, the best approach is to start at the higher-level decision-makers and not to start at the middle management that has no powers. Once the top guy likes the idea, he'll empower the lower guys to work with me. This way, the middle-management guy is now safe and protected as well as instructed to work on the idea with me. If he is not enthusiastic, I can always report to the top guy again and ask for another working partner. To keep him motivated, I always cc every email to the top guy so that the middle guy is aware that he is being monitored. Both carrots and sticks are needed, but finding the right person is the key to navigating the maze of bureaucrazy.

So how do we get the top guy aligned to the innovative idea? Identify the right decision-maker who can benefit from the success of the innovative idea, and frame the narrative of the idea in alignment with his aspirations to incentivize him. It takes a lot of research, trial and error, and luck to eventually meet the right person at the top who is interested. I have to keep trying multiple ideas and with multiple people. If I try hundred ideas, ten might become immediately plausible, the rest are at different stages of ripening, and one or two might be implemented every year. From ideation to implementation, an idea might take anywhere between one year to twenty-five years. I need to be patient and wait for it to happen.

So next time you are angry with the government, think of how to mobilize them. It takes hard work and lots of trying, but a constructive approach is better than fighting and protesting. Fighting is not the easy way out, and it is definitely not the easy way in. I've also seen many peers suffer when they adopted confrontational clashes just to reach futile damages. Frictions are heat losses and harmony is bliss. I've become a loving critic instead. My dean at LKYSPP was Kishore Mahbubani. He taught me to frame my arguments and narratives properly. I need to have a plan and a purpose before I start. Don't waste your effort going all over the place. Make a strategy worth your effort if you really want change to happen.

On graduation day, I was fifty-six. I rented a Mandarin Official Hat from the Chinese operas costume shop and took this shot (see page 11) in the toilet of the graduation hall as a potential qualified bureaucrat. I had to travel so much that my two-year course took four years to complete. The LKYSPP closed down its part-time courses the year I graduated. I'm glad I caught the last train home.

Through this process, I learned that frustration is a form of energy that can be converted into positive and constructive energy. All I need to do is to be calm, collect my thoughts, and envision the pathways to a better future. Confrontations and frictions are heat loss and should be only used as a last resort when everything else has failed to achieve the greater good.

Lesson:

Don't get upset with bureaucrats. The system of bureaucrazy is designed to resist change, and to make you give up trying new ideas. Try to navigate the system to find the pathways and people who can facilitate the change needed. It is a tedious and humbling process, but with patience and some luck, it can be done. Pressure can be used when there is no progress. That includes social media to rally popular demand.

The bureaucrat is paid by taxpayers' money to do his job. He is not paid to try. He is paid to deliver.

Lifelong Learning and Teaching

My lack of a degree in my earlier years led me to a voracious hunger for knowledge. I took a wide range of short courses from management to real estate marketing, union leadership, listening skills, and photography. I even took drum classes so that I could join a band but failed as I travelled too often to regularly attend them.

I also expanded my knowledge through my travels to sixty-four countries and hundreds of cities, with multiple trips to many of them. For all my lifelong learnings, I was given the Skills Future Fellowship Award by our President Halimah Yacob in 2022, with an SGD 10,000 prize to continue learning. (See appendix for the list for the courses I took.)

Some tips for learning:

1. **Never stop asking questions.** I failed everything in school, so I kept on learning, reading, and asking impertinent questions. I've seen many educated people stop asking new questions and they stagnate over time.

2. **Be open to learning from anyone, anywhere, anytime.** As someone who's older, I mix with young people because they remind me of the endless possibilities of the changing world in terms of technology, AI, and culture. If you are humble, you can learn more. If you are defensive, it can prevent you from learning important things.

3. **Learning is more fun when you can see how to apply it.** I learn random things that are seemingly unrelated to my work. But this wide range of random knowledge allows me to learn in cross-disciplinary patterns. It's like having a much larger toolbox than others.

The first time I was attending an Executive Course at Harvard Business School in Cambridge, USA, I noticed the class interaction was totally different from Singapore classrooms. Whenever a question was asked, I saw about 20 per cent of the class wanted to answer. In Singapore, the students tend to wait for someone else to answer. I asked the Harvard professor how he did it. He said the students want to answer when they know the answer, because it is unlikely that I pick the same person twice.

He also told me his teaching formula: Since every student is expected to have read the cases, he only has to highlight the key points for discussions. He teaches 20 per cent of content. The students teach each other 40 per cent of the expected content through their answers. The trick is to trigger them to speak up spontaneously. If the students can suggest experimental ideas in class without the fear of being ridiculed, new ideas can emerge and be debated. In many classrooms, lots of good thoughts were suppressed when the students feared saying 'stupid things'. In a safe space, there is no such thing as a stupid idea.

When I graduated with a Master's in Public Administration, I became an Adjunct Associate Professor at the National University of Singapore. My first class was not in Singapore but to teach a two-week social entrepreneurship module at the College of Management Academic Studies (COMAS), which was the largest college in Israel.

It was my first time teaching formally. My class consisted of sixteen adult MBA students who started at 4 p.m. every day after work and ended at 10 p.m. each night. They were tired and I was unable to energize them with the boring formal curriculum. After two hours, I decided to dump the curriculum and ask them about their lives. Everyone in the class got to know each other and me. I told them about my journey from sixteen companies to becoming Mr Toilet, the Social Entrepreneur. They asked me questions non-stop for the rest of the course and each night, they went home more energized at 10 p.m. than they were at 4 p.m. One of them had an uncle who owned a cactus farm and, on the weekend, we all drove in a few cars to visit the farm and learn how his uncle operated the farm profitably. On the following Monday, I got the students to teach the farmers of Ethiopian Cactus Farmers Association online, and the Ethiopian farmers found it very useful to learn how Israeli cactus farms are more efficient than theirs. I realized that students loved real-world lessons and they also loved to share.

At the end of the course, the students wrote to the principal of the school that this was the best module of their entire MBA course, and this module itself was worth the fees they paid for the whole course. I was, of course, flattered.

Three months later, my friends from the Ethiopian Cactus Farmers Association told me some of the students are still giving them free consultancy to improve their business.

I told my students that just like them, I knew everything, except the things I didn't know. When I don't know, I google and know everything again. Now with Generative AI, knowledge is not the power any more. The ability to understand the problems, envision the desired outcomes, and prompt the right questions become the keys to success. Rote learning is archaic and quite useless now. Learning is an everyday thing not limited to formal studies. And now when I teach in universities, I love telling stories and also learning from my students.

Lessons:

Enquiry is the seed of genius. Keep asking questions, dreaming ideas, imagining scenarios, fantasizing a better future, challenging norms, asking 'What if', and don't hold back your thoughts. If you feel your thoughts are too raw, you can write them down, ponder and refine them a bit before openly asking for feedback. If you keep the habit of enquiry, your speed of thinking will break through your past thoughts and strengthen your brain muscles continuously.

Education: The Plantation vs the Rainforest

School operates like a plantation.

We seat our uniformed kids in uniform rows, give them lessons in uniformity and fertilize them with the same textbooks. The classroom looks like an organized rows of cabbages. Every child is given instructions clearly and systematically and they are tested on what is taught. They are never tested on implementing what they're not taught. We do not reward students who learn outside the curriculum, and we reward conformity as the way to success. Everything is supposed to be neat and tidy. In the process, the imagination of the child narrows to what they are incentivized to study.

Uniformity protects the teachers and principals from any accusation of being biased and so qualitative subjects like entrepreneurship, imagination, and challenging norms are seen as misfits. Many scholars become holders of higher management positions or political office, but they may not have the qualities needed for society. Many end up with a false sense of superiority and arrogance, yet are unable to gain respect from others.

The plantation is fragile. All bugs are killed by toxic pesticides. Both good bugs and bad bugs are fumigated or sprayed upon. Good ideas are also fumigated.

The school becomes a place that stifles the multiple talents of the child by measuring him only in one single dimension. And the child learns never to challenge the authorities.

Now, what if society really was like a rainforest?

The child enters a state of shock when he enters society. It is no more a farm. Instead, in the rainforest, most of the rules of the plantation do not apply any more. Plants are not growing in uniformity. The rainforest looks untidy, but it derives its resilience from its biodiversity. Each plant, bug, animal, and bird supports the ecosystem sustainably: a symbiosis that never existed in the plantation.

The child has to unlearn what he learned at the plantation and relearn how to survive in the forest.

You may do well in the plantation but it doesn't prepare you for the rainforest. That's why so many of us live in conformity and fear, and cannot innovate outside the box.

We need talents who can mobilize resources across disciplines and sectors, and to achieve this, we need a wholesomely educated child. Once he is educated in a spherical manner, and not linear, he can see patterns where others see chaos.

This is where their survival instinct does the catching up.

Lee Kuan Yew said this in the parliament in 1977: 'My definition of an educated man is a man who never stops learning and wants to learn. I am not interested in whether a man has a PhD or not, or an MA for that matter, or a diploma. Mao never had one, neither had Khrushchev, nor Stalin.'[34]

Without an all-round education, we will not be competitive.

The solutions for the revamping of our educational system are as follows:

1. Businesses have to change the way they recruit talents based on their ability to deliver outcomes and not purely based on their paper qualifications. This will bring workers with multiple talents, including a healthy blend of soft skills and hard skills.

2. Businesses can work with the Ministry of Education to educate parents and students that their future career prospects depend on both their soft skills and hard skills. This will drive the parents to help their children with their curiosity, courage, compassion, commitment, communication, collaboration, and their sense of community to prepare for future life. This will also disrupt the exam-oriented tuition industry accordingly.

3. If education is focused on the joy of learning, we could migrate from a fear-based educational system to a love-based educational system, which is less stressful for everyone.

Education should not be defined nor limited by grades. Education can happen inside and outside the classroom. It is happening at home, in the streets, on social media, in extracurricular activities, in nature, travels, books, movies, sports, relaxation, social interaction, conferences, work, and play.

Lessons:

Overly focusing on grades can create conformists and stifle the genius in every child. Education is holistic. Learning by doing activates the head, heart, and hands to make the learning experience real and fun.

We need to migrate from our current fear-based education to love-based education. From fear of failing to cultivating a can-do attitude in every child.

The Tech Gap: Singularity University

I kept hearing about Silicon Valley and its start-up culture, which was always portrayed as the coolest place where new technologies and business models were born. I was still clueless when in 2014, Darlene Damm of Singularity University called me to go to Silicon Valley to deliver a lecture. They needed to orientate the tech students on how social entrepreneurs can use technology to improve society. They flew me to the NASA Campus in Mountain View, San Francisco, where I met eighty young students and stayed with them for two days.

I was curious to learn more, so in 2016, when they offered full scholarships, I applied. The acceptance rate was only 0.5 per cent, even lower than the 3.4 per cent chance of getting into Harvard. The interview panellists told me that since I was not a technologist, the course might not be suitable for me. I told them that since the class was full of technologists, they needed a serial entrepreneur and serial social entrepreneur to balance the mutual learning of the class. Afterall, tech needs business models and I can be very helpful for the class. I told them I hope to use their technologies to end poverty for 4 billion poor people. They accepted my story and I spent ten weeks living with seventy-nine other young people with ages ranging from twenty-two to forty. I was the oldest at fifty-nine, and they called me Grandpa. It was the first time I experienced campus life and it's a very memorable part of my life.

From Day 1, they told us we were selected because we were misfits and innovators who challenged the norms, and we should now think at an exponential scale, using technology to solve and improve the lives of a billion people.

I had a lot of difficulties grasping all the technological terms, until I realized some of the others were also having similar challenges. They brought us to site visits, threw lots of parties, trained us to design pitch decks, and even funded us if our presentation was plausible.

My team called Clinicai pitched for a smart toilet that would be able to diagnose colorectal cancer using spectral cameras and a nano-nose licensed to us by NASA, used in the space station. We won USD 100,000 investment from Singularity University, and IndieBio, a biotech incubator, also invested another USD 225,000 in us. Another USD 50,000 came from the Taiwanese Tech Assistance grant. In total, we raised USD 375,000. We achieved the Minimum Viable Product, but were unable to attract large-scale funding for clinical trials. We decided to close it down a few years later.

I learned so much in this journey and became conversant with start-up culture.

One of my favourite teachers was Salim Ismail who taught us exponential organization. I learned how to marry technologies with my leverage model. It influenced my exponential mindset in eradicating global poverty at a billion-impact level.

We had 200 teachers and 400 mentors, and they taught us about the highest-level technologies, including biotechnology,

3D printing, med-tech, sensors, robotics, blockchain, crypto currency, artificial intelligence, machine learning, biomimicry, genetic engineering, cellular farming, nanobots, hyperspectral imaging, virtual reality, renewable energy, cyber security, quantum computing, Generative AI and Artificial General Intelligence—the list goes on.

I was shocked to learn that every one of these technologies is going to replace human resources at a very rapid pace and they are anti-jobs technologies. Whether it's airport self check-in or McDonald's self-order or self-driving fork-lift or chatbots replacing millions of call centre operators, these technological meteorites are going to strike the planet in an unprecedented blast of joblessness. Even though there are many jobs for highly skilled technology workers right now, the current workforce is not skilled enough to take on those jobs and the mismatch of jobs and skills will explode since our educational system is still not changing to adapt to this new situation. With the speed of Generative AI, the danger of Generative AI growing rapidly while the educational system is lagging far behind, social and political upheaval is expected when the people suffer economically.

Lesson:

Technology is increasing at the speed of geometrical progression, whereas the educational system worldwide has stagnated since the last century. Even the measurement of PISA, QS World University Rankings, or Times Higher Education Rankings are all based on archaic metrics that are quite irrelevant in the age of Generative Artificial Intelligence. As knowledge becomes commoditized by prompt engineering, asking questions is now more important than remembering answers. Rote-learning is now obsolete.

The Fourth Industrial Revolution

If I had not gone to Singularity University, I would still be complacent and unaware of the issues to do with this technological growth.

So, how do we prepare ourselves and our children for this anti-jobs future that is called the Fourth Industrial Revolution?

Every sector of the society is due for disruption. Hotels challenged by Airbnb. Taxis are challenged by Uber and Grab. Chatbots taking over call-centre workers. AI taking over journalists, script-writers, actors, musicians, etc. If employers can use robots who can work 24/7, 365 days, they would prefer not to employ humans. If machine learning can make things cheaper, faster, better, and easier, who needs humans? Large Language Models are the algorithmic basis for chatbots like GPT-4 and Google's Bard. Its accuracy has improved exponentially. Technology is like an extension of our brain power. Our educational system has to migrate from learning knowledge to learning how to use technology.

As I sat through the ten-week course at Singularity, it dawned on me that it is not the technology I should be

290 The Gumption of Mr Toilet

worried about. These technologies are transient; they, too, will become obsolete and be replaced with newer ones. And new technologies appear because someone has the imagination to create them. What is constant is my ability to mobilize them as they emerge. This is the result of my entrepreneurial skill set. This means that beyond hard skills, what we need to teach in schools are soft skills such as:

- Curiosity to question
- Courage to imagine and implement; entrepreneurial dare
- Commitment to complete challenging and tedious tasks
- Compassion to empathize with all people: customers, colleagues, bosses, and the world at large. The power of love is infectious to boosting teamwork.
- Collaboration: The ability to mobilize others into win-win alignments; the humility to let others shine.
- Community: To be able to identify and use an 'ecosystem approach' to solutions instead of thinking only in fragmented silos.
- Communication skills to inform, equip, convince, and motivate actions by others.

Every child needs this list of 7Cs to survive the future. Because these are the seeds of genius that can create leaders in every field.

Rote-learning and memory tests are the domains of the robot. Our PISA score is high in Singapore, but PISA, QS Universities Ranking, and Times Higher Education World University Rankings are all archaic measurement tools that are already obsolete, and yet, our parents are still pressure-cooking their kids to get better grades in the hope of giving them a head start in life. It's sad to see their investments go to waste. The only benefit of going to a prestigious school is probably to build a network of future successful friends, but that is not a guarantee any more.

We should depart from a tendency to emphasize these in the education system and move towards unleashing the untapped gifts in every child.

Humans have spirituality, morals, ethics, aesthetics, philosophy, and love. Our future competitiveness against robots lies in these human virtues. Our ability to care, love, and imagine will allow us to continue to be masters of robots, and not their servants.

The global educational model has been focused on finding the right answers to questions. This way of education is not competitive in the Fourth Industrial Revolution today.

In the age of artificial intelligence, where answers are easily available, the educational system should focus on asking questions instead. To be clear, asking the right questions does not guarantee the right answers. Instead, when children are trained to ask questions continually, their inquisitive minds will open up to more and better answers.

The educational system needs to be shifted into a system of inquiries to teach children how to survive. Parents cannot teach their children how to predict examination questions by sending them to tuition or answering past examination questions.

Regurgitation of correct answers will not be valued in a world where GPT and other apps can give the answers. One's skill will now depend on one's depth of questioning, ability to sift through the myriad of potential answers and opportunities, and then applying them to solve context-specific problems.

This method of education is not new. Jewish children are taught by their parents every day before going to school to ask questions of their teachers. This ethnic group has produced at least 20 per cent of all Nobel prize winners. I visited a Kibbutz school in Israel and was received by a boy of twelve and a girl of nine. They gave me a tour of their school and explained how their teachers do not teach them. They were taught to learn by themselves in class by discussing the books with each other. Their teachers only facilitated questions and procured supply of tools/equipment upon requests by the students. I visited the Democratic School in Israel and saw that students could learn from any class at any level they wished, e.g., they could decide to study math, science, English, etc. at different grades according to their personal speed of learning.

At another model called Univer-City, students learn from the city instead of the classrooms. The school can organize visits to any government departments, companies, civil society organizations or parks, and places that the students requested as long as the initiatives are taken by the students who will interview these organizations and the students might also propose to them new ideas of improvements as well.

To get students fit for the future, our educational system needs to give students the courage and audacity to imagine future possibilities, and seek answers to create the future in their visions. We need to help them overcome their imposter syndrome of feeling anxious and doubting their abilities.

Students will take ownership of their learning process, and teachers will be retrained to become facilitators to nurture a new generation of interdisciplinary thinkers and doers. This has to be part of the national culture.

Above all, we need to nurture socio-emotional intelligence in children so that they can grow up to become compassionate people who care about others.

Lesson:

We need such an educational system and break the mould of previous methods if parents, educationalists, employers, technologists, and the authorities are aligned on what needs to be done. We need them to openly educate each other to design our future.

SUCCESSES, FAILURES, AND
WORKS IN PROGRESS

Solving Human Trafficking in
Singapore's Construction Industry

Singapore ranks third in the list of least corrupt countries in
the world, just behind Denmark and Norway, but is considered
a corruption-free country where you can live your entire life
without having to pay a single bribe to any government official.
However, corruption can be imported, because it happened
over other countries with impact in Singapore. For the last
thirty years, it is public knowledge that the mafias in India and
Bangladesh have been overcharging the construction workers
between one to two years of their wages to arrange them to
come and work in Singapore.

I felt that this was a very inhumane practice that must be
stopped. I met our new Minister for National Development,
Desmond Lee, and suggested to him that it's time to break
this human trafficking problem. I convinced him that while
this is intricate to resolve, it is possible if he instructs the
Building Control Authority (BCA) to work with me until it is
solved. Even though the malpractices are done in Bangladesh
and India, they have to be solved if Singapore wants to be

blemish-free as a buyer of their services. He liked that vision and agreed to give the endeavour his full support.

For the supply side, BoP Hub partnered with BRAC, the biggest NGO in Bangladesh to replace the mafia. BRAC recruited, trained, and processed the workers to come into Singapore. We partnered with the Asia Philanthropy Circle (APC), a foundation that funded the secretariat staff, to follow up on action every week.

I'm very glad that APC did a meticulous job chasing everyone into action and took deep ownership of this project. We brought APC, BCA, and the Ministry of Manpower (MOM) to visit Bangladesh and this system change process took four years to create a pilot sandbox approved by both BCA and the MOM. Employers can now find their workers directly, bypassing the mafia. BCA told us that they're also working to solve the same problem with other partners from other countries. This means we have succeeded in system change beyond our own effort and now spreading into India, Myanmar, Sri Lanka, and other countries.

There are about 300,000 migrant construction workers in Singapore. If this new system is eventually completely implemented, the workers will be able to collectively send home SGD 2 to 3 billion extra money to send their kids to school, build a better house, and eat better nutrition. This is a life-changing system for them.

We are now looking to see if this model can also be applicable for the UAE and other receiving countries. We did not make any money. Our reward has been to see a fairer world for the disadvantaged people. It is gratifying to see the new badges of workers coming into Singapore through BRAC, directly bypassing the mafia.

45Rice brand (pronounced as Fortified Rice)

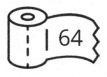

45Rice

I read a report in 2015 that our 300,000 foreign construction workers (mainly from India and Bangladesh) were not getting sufficient nutrition in their daily meals. I immediately remembered attending a seminar where the Dutch vitamin company DSM was explaining how they work with Food and Agriculture Organization (FAO) to supply fortified rice to the poor to gain their needed nutrients through their rice intake. I thought this could be the solution for these under-nourished construction workers. I flew to the Netherlands to persuade the Director of DSM to invest SGD 100,000 to set up a small factory to extrude fortified rice. I told him this would work as if he gave me a free colour printer on the condition that I buy cartridges from him forever. If he gave me the machines, I'd buy the raw materials forever. He agreed and sent me a letter with conditions that we needed to reach a certain level of order before the grant would be released.

I used the letter and raised an SGD 500,000 convertible loan from raiSE, our government's social enterprise platform, and created a new start-up called 45Rice (pronounced as Fortified

Rice) providing nutritious meals to foreign construction workers in Singapore.[35] I appointed a General Manager and gave him shares to operate the company in 2016.

We sold more than 1 million meals with this fortified rice in the first year. However, the business was not profitable as the construction workers were very price-sensitive and the impact of the nutrition improvements is a slow process and is not instantly visible. We wanted to charge 5 cents more per meal but were unable to fetch any higher price per meal than the normal meals sold by current caterers. 45Rice ran out of funds and we had to close it down in the third year.

A visually impaired guide briefing his sighted
participants on their tour in total darkness

Dialogue in the Dark Singapore

When I first saw the Dialogue in the Dark Museum in Davos at the World Economic Forum 2006, it was an amazing new experience simulating blindness by walking in total darkness guided by a blind guide who become 'sighted' and I become 'blind' since I had to rely on his voice to guide me throughout the one-hour journey. This experience opened up my empathy and appreciation for the survival skills of blind people.

I told Andreas Heinecke, the founder of Dialogue in the Dark, that I'd like to set up a permanent DiD museum in Singapore.

My attempts to bring it to Singapore were rejected by both the Singapore Science Centre and the Singapore Discovery Centre.

After two years of trying unsuccessfully to find a suitable location and investors, I received an invitation from Andreas to join their international meeting for all the DiD centres in twenty cities. I interviewed a visually impaired guy called Han Wee Ong and invited him to come to Holon, Israel, for the meeting and training. I paid for his trip and also brought my twelve-year-old daughter, Earth Sim, for the experience.

At Holon, each city representative gave an update and when I was on stage, they asked me why I had come so early bringing a potential guide for training since I still did not have a venue in Singapore yet. I replied that I had to behave as if it was going to happen so that it might happen for real. The audience was astonished at such a foolhardy response, but gave a very enthusiastic applause for my spirit. I was doing something purely based on a belief that it'll somehow eventually happen.

Upon my return to Singapore, I sold the idea to the principal of Ngee Ann Polytechnic that since Ngee Ann Polytechnic has a Diploma in Social Enterprise course, this could become a practical training business that the students could operate as part of their practicum. He loved it and after exhausting all space options, he decided to demolish two seminar rooms to provide for the 4,000 square feet needed for the museum. Together, we raised SGD 1 million government grants to bring in the German franchise and construct the Dialogue in the Dark Singapore, which opened in 2009. Each year, we attract 20,000 paid visitors and employ seventeen visually impaired individuals as guides. Han Wee became a trainer and has been an executive for fifteen years now. It became the most financially sustainable Dialogue in the Dark museum in the world because the operating labour cost is low and we don't have to pay rent.

I highly recommend you to visit any of the Dialogue in the Dark Museum in the world. The experience is life-changing and you will never see a blind person in the same way you see them now.

Designing Toilet Exhibitions

After gaining the experience of setting up Dialogue in the Dark, I met the Singapore Science Centre and proposed to have a toilet exhibition. They told me that I could do such a show two years later after one of their current exhibitions ended. I started working on a fun learning journey of a toilet exhibition myself. I studied the types of poop on the Bristol Stool Chart. I studied the nature of farts and why it is so necessary in our digestive process. I studied all kinds of intestinal worms, including hookworms, ringworms, tapeworms, pinworms, whipworms, etc. when I received a call from an exhibition centre in Limburg in the Netherlands who wanted me to be their consultant to design a toilet exhibition. I jumped at the opportunity and we launched the 'Everything You Always Wanted to Know About Toilets' exhibition in 2018 at the Cube Design Museum.

I returned to co-design the 'Know Your Poo' exhibition at the Singapore Science Centre, and we launched it in 2019, depicting the journey of Singapore's progress through the improvements of our toilets, from the British Bucket System, to Flush Toilets, to Deep Tunnel Sewage System, to NEWater, the filtered safe drinking water from our toilet. The exhibition was so popular, it is still running after six years and is planned to stay for four more years.

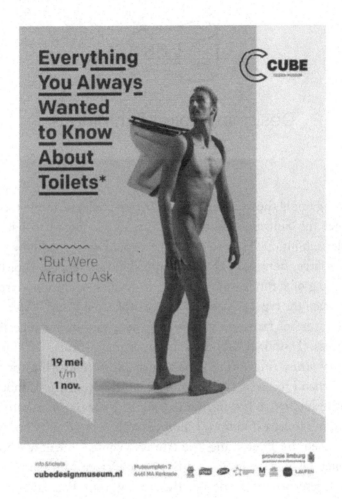

Poster for the exhibition in Limburg, Netherlands

Poster for the Singapore Science Centre exhibition

World Toilet Museum concept by JAJA Architect, Denmark

World Toilet Museum

The World Toilet Museum is an initiative advocating a rebranding of toilets from being a taboo to a status symbol and an object of desire. To do so, the museum is not only supporting public education of sanitation, it will become a toilet and sanitation attraction—a tourist destination.

I wished to create a museum that is dedicated to representing this diversity. A museum that is full of learning, experimenting, and inventing experiences, unveiling all aspects of toilets and sanitation.

I met the owner of JAJA Architect from Denmark during a cocktail dinner at Copenhagen, and told him of my dream. He got inspired and went on to develop this stunning architectural form looking like three toilet rolls from the aerial view. The three loops are the Evolution Loop, the Culture Loop, and the Process Loop.

The Evolution Loop shows visitors the milestones in the evolution of the toilet and gives them an insight into the importance of sanitation and its effect on world history. Visitors walk along a path that is aligned with decorated and themed rooms according to a certain historical period. They can go on a trip through history by entering a roman privy room, looking at a mediaeval tower toilet or exploring future outer space toilets.

The Culture Loop invites visitors on a journey around the world and they can experience the diversity of toilet cultures. Visitors will learn about the different sanitation habits and policies of our global society. A row of toilet booths along the inner façade of the loop features toilet designs and typologies from around the world.

The Process Loop shows visitors the flow of the sanitation cycle. Visitors will get an understanding of the different technologies and their impact on the environment. The loop does not only explain current practices, it also provides information on research topics and new technologies. The tour starts with the processes in the human body, continues with the functionality of the toilet and sanitation system, the water treatment and composting process, and ends with the by-products and their re-entry into the sanitation cycle.

So far, I've proposed it to the Hainan Provincial government. They needed tourism products but our studies of their tourists' demographics show that the Russian and Chinese tourists are beach and sun lovers, and a museum of this kind will not appeal to them.

I'm still looking for the right location and investors for this World Toilet Museum. This needs to be a government initiative in order to sustain the operations as a public good, as a tourist attraction, and an educational centre.

Singapore Batik

Transforming food to fashion

In 2025, Singapore will celebrate its sixtieth National Day but we still do not have a national dress. In fact, we also find it difficult to describe the Singaporean identity. With a short history, it has a cosmopolitan population of 75.9 per cent Chinese, 15.4 per cent Malays, 7.4 per cent Indians, 1.6 per cent other races, and a continuous influx of new citizens, residents, and tourists from hundreds of other ethnicities.[36] As a young nation of immigrants, we practice the festivals, cultures, and rituals from the original lands of our forefathers. To truly become a nation, it is imperative that we need a unifying identity to avoid becoming a 'hotel' instead of attaining nationhood.

There were a few past attempts to create a Singapore national dress but none have succeeded in gaining acceptance and nobody wants to wear them. To be successful, we have to capture the DNA of Singaporeans. The Singapore Airlines uniform is the most famous Singapore batik but it is a uniform.

I focused on developing design language for our three most prominent unique intimacies:

1. Hawker Culture in Singapore was successfully inscribed as Singapore's first element on the UNESCO Representative List of the Intangible Cultural Heritage of Humanity on 16 December 2020.
2. Our Singlish, an informal, colloquial mixture of English, Malay, and Chinese dialects, which is intimately our common local language.
3. Eighty per cent of Singaporeans live in public housing called HDB Flats. This is the largest financial investment of Singaporeans.

My dream is to have everyone, including our Cabinet Ministers and parliamentarians, dress up in this national dress on 9 August at our annual National Day Parade to launch it. I spoke to our Minister of State for the Ministry of Culture, Community and Youth recently and he likes the idea. I want to create a legacy for a uniquely Singapore Batik that is distinctly identifiable from any other batik that has existed in other lands. I'm working with the Raffles College of Higher Education to organize a national design contest so that our young designers might produce the first series of our SG Batik. If the Indonesians can clearly differentiate their batik from Bali, Yogyakarta, Madura, Sulawesi, and Java, certainly Singapore can have its distinctive design language too. I have now assembled a young team of designers and also started applying for grants for this project.

When successful, we can exile all the western jackets from Singapore. The western jacket was a temperate climate dress unsuitable for the tropical climate of Singapore. It was a symbol of colonialism here. The indoor temperature in many of our commercial buildings is now freezing cold as low as 22°C and ladies have to even bring shawls to their wintry cold offices. We can set the temperature higher if nobody (the bosses, lawyers, real estate agents, etc.) wears jackets in the offices. For general comfort in Singapore when wearing summer clothes, we can tune to 24°C or 25°C. This will save us lots of energy. In Japan, there already is a Coolbiz law that all buildings should be 25°C in summer and nobody should wear a tie.

I hope we can promote the first series of SG batik designs by many artists so that Singapore will have its own unique national dress just like our neighbouring countries.

Everybody's Business

Everybody's Business Movie Poster

I wanted to make a movie about the plight of the people who didn't have toilets in India. Having no experience, I googled 'how to make a movie'. There were sixteen steps starting with writing a story, converting to script, getting a producer, director, funding, casting, recce, shooting, editing, distribution, promotion, etc. There was too much to learn.

George Yeo introduced me to the famous Singapore Director/Producer Jack Neo and I asked him how one could write a good story. Over two hours of coffee chat, he taught me about creating a story arc with ups and downs, creating a key character from zero to hero, creating situational comedy, creating supporting characters, and wrapping up with a happy ending.

I sent him a story after a week and met him again. Titled 'Life Without Toilets', it was about how each of the six members of an Indian family—the protagonist, his wife, his daughter, his mother, and his twin sons—suffered when their house did not have a toilet. The story includes challenges, comedy, corruption, love story, conflicts, and reconciliations, and I also wrote six songs' lyrics to include Bollywood dancing scenes. Jack Neo liked the story but he was afraid to go to India to shoot a movie as he was unfamiliar with the country.

So, I wrote a new movie story about public toilets in Singapore and how twenty-two food poisoning cases were spread from dirty coffee shop toilets. He liked it again and I went to pitch it to our Infocomm Media Development Authority who funded SGD 1 million. I guess the name of Jack Neo made it easier to get funded. He brought his usual cast of local popular comedians including Gurmit Singh as a Hygiene Officer, Drag Queen Kumar as the Minister of Toilet, and Mark Lee, Liu Ling Ling, Wang Lei, Henry Chia, and many others. We shot it in a coffee shop at North Bridge Rd, and some other studios. The script by Boris Boo was changed many times by Jack Neo during shooting. But he kept my movie title 人人有份 in Mandarin, which has a double meaning: 'Everyone has Shit' as well as 'Everyone has Duty'. The English name 'Everybody's Business' also contained a pun as 'doing business' is a euphemism for pooping. On the poster, it says 'Original Story Concept by Jack Sim'.

We booked the entire Golden Harvest cinema at VivoCity on the opening night in 2013, and sold charity fundraising tickets at SGD 50 per ticket. It was a very nice feeling to realize you don't need to be an expert to do anything. Just talk to some experts, google, and do it. And now with Generative AI, it is so much easier to be whoever you want to be without prior deep expertise.

The movie was ranked within the Top 10 of Chinese movies in Singapore but fell out of the chart within a short time as other Chinese movies took the screens.

It was fun to be able to create yet another avenue to amplify my toilet stories and I want to do more movies in future.

Commemorating Lee Kuan Yew

My childhood dream was to be an artist and these surges of creative juices keep emerging. I did a few pieces and here is one of them:

Lee Kuan Yew's Bust

Lee Kuan Yew belongs to an exclusive group of Fathers of Nations alongside Mustafa Kemal Atatürk of Turkey, Nelson Mandela of South Africa, Mahatma Gandhi of India, Tunku Abdul Rahman of Malaysia, Sun Yat-sen of China, Sukarno of Indonesia, Ho Chi Minh of Vietnam, and others.

Like many Singaporean baby boomers (born between 1946 and 1964), I found Lee Kuan Yew to be a major inspiration in my life. To be living through his lifetime was a privilege, watching him transform our lives from poverty to prosperity, and knowing that this can be done for other countries as well.

On the SG50, Singapore's fiftieth National Day, in 2015, I wanted to make a bronze sculpture of Lee Kuan Yew. I couldn't sculpt, but I could draw. I must have looked at nearly hundreds of his photos in different poses and times. Each time, he exuded the spirit of a deep thinker and a brave confident fighter. I wanted to create a robust image portraying the steel and gumption inside him. His forehead was of particular prominence to me. Designing this bust was like a problem-solving process. It started with conservative sketches, which I modified, and it evolved through trial and error until it reached a point of satisfaction. I sent my sketches to a workshop in Bangkok, Thailand, to have them produced into a 3D digital model. After many iterations, I went there myself. I was very satisfied with the final mould and we casted a series of bronze busts of LKY. I gave one each to my alma maters, namely Whitley Secondary School, three ITE Colleges, and the Lee Kuan Yew School of Public Policy. I also gave one to George Yeo as a token of gratitude for his continuous support.

On the hundredth anniversary of Lee Kuan Yew's birthday, this sculpture was displayed at the LKY Experience to tell his life story and for the public to see for nine months, with lots of visitors enjoying the bust.

I still have several pieces in my house for future use. Bronze and Lee Kuan Yew, they last forever.

A bastion of the Fort Tanjong Katong buried in Katong Park

Conserving Heritage: Fort Tanjong Katong

When I moved into my Meyer Road house in 1992, I was curious why the adjacent road was named Fort Rd. I asked an old neighbour and he told me there was a fort somewhere around here before, but I could not find it.

In 2001, the outline of the top of the bastion wall became visible during a dry spell when all the grass was gone. This prompted me to seek out the relevant authorities to investigate its origins. The National Archives of Singapore investigated with the London Metropolitan Archives and found the plans of Fort Tanjong Katong! It stood from 1879 to 1901, and was one of the oldest military forts built by the former British colonial government of Singapore. Due to land reclamation, the fort was buried by Katong Park as the reclamation continued to build the East Coast Highway and the East Coast Beach. In short, the beach has moved from the fort to more than 1 kilometre away!

I lobbied our Member of Parliament Andy Gan to resurrect the fort and he agreed.

In 2004, a community-based project named 'Raising History, Planting Roots' was initiated by the Mountbatten Citizens' Consultative Committee with local residents and schools as a community involvement programme to encourage ownership of local heritage. In just four weeks, an amount of SGD 200,000 was raised from corporate sponsors and a fundraising dinner, with former Prime Minister Goh Chok Tong, was held.

However, I was disappointed that after digging up the sprawling fort, with massive media publicity, they reburied it again as the government had no plans to expose it further. They told me it was only rocks. I told them we would go to Europe to see their monuments and ruins and we'd never call their monumental ruins 'rocks'.

As a protest, I designed and built two concrete statues of Red British Guards and placed them along Fort Rd to remind people of the fort there. The NParks gave me permission after it was built, and it became a permanent monument there. It was more like forgiveness than permission but that was the easier way to get it approved.

After more than thirty years of lobbying for the preservation of this heritage monument, with the new Member of Parliament Lim Biow Chuan, the National Parks agreed to build a café at the park to educate people about the existence of the fort. A portion will be exposed and the rest will have ground markers showing the outlines of the fort. The Katong Park MRT train station opens in 2024 next to the fort.

The patience needed for this project was really enduring and tiring, but I knew that if I don't give up, something good will prevail.

The Need for Local Public Arts

Whenever I am overseas, I take the opportunity to visit the local art galleries and to walk in the streets to see their public arts. The culture of a city is often revealed in its public arts and architecture. However, in the case of Singapore, most of our skyscrapers are signature buildings designed by world-renowned foreign architects, and our public artworks also by world-renowned artists. There is a certain thinking here that in order to be an international city, everything has to be done by famous international designers. This created a biblical problem where prophets are not welcome at home. Although Singaporean architects and artists are designing major works in China and other countries, few are invited to build monumental projects at home. To provoke new mindsets, artists sometimes need to be rebels to take ownership of our local public spaces.

My zebra crossing

The standard zebra crossing

I made this zebra crossing and proposed it to our Land Transport Authority giving several good reasons. Firstly, Singapore's tourism promotion would gain from free global publicity when tourists and visitors post selfies and photos of themselves with our unique zebra crossing. Secondly, it would promote creativity when citizens start thinking openly and come up with even more new ideas. Lastly, the current design was wrong. It was straight bands and not zebra bands. Therefore, it needed to be corrected to be called zebra crossing.

I called a journalist and the article went into mainstream newspapers. But the LTA wrote a warning letter to me to remove it or face penalties.

Having achieved my media stunt, I removed it immediately. I hoped it planted a seed in the minds of some Singaporeans to think outside the box.

Two years later, I painted a giraffe design on a public lamp post outside my house. It stayed there for about three months and one morning, they simply repainted it back in the original silver colour, without any discussion.

I saw a pair of grey bollard concrete blocks covered with algae outside my house and painted it into an oriental lotus design. The Land Transport Authority received a complaint that I had vandalized the bollock and asked me to repaint it to the original grey colour. I showed him a photo of the original grey stained bollard and asked him which one looked better. He said obviously the painted one looked better, but technically it was vandalism. I told him that I'd write to the National Arts Council (NAC) and propose a public art contest to beautify all the bollards on the island. He liked the idea and said he'll make that report and close the case for now. I wrote to the NAC with such a proposal and did not get any reply. So, the painted bollards remain.

There were a few other graffiti artists who were punished for vandalism, which means destruction or damaging public properties. I appreciate that they didn't see my works as vandalism and send me to jail. Instead, they were seen as unauthorized artworks. I felt I've made my case and the media story is already out there.

I will continue to take the risk to push the envelope for a more creative society with my benign provocations.

I wish my country could be more open-minded to allow and encourage more local public arts in Singapore, like other culturally matured countries do. I love my country more than I love the rules.

My painted bollard vs bare bollard

Think Equal

Singapore is a multicultural, multiracial, and multireligious nation of migrants, with high income disparity. Racial and religious harmony is one of the cornerstones of Singapore's positioning as a safe and progressive nation. To prevent discrimination, racism, and xenophobia, we need to teach kids empathy from the beginning, at age four or five, to be resilient against prejudices of skin colours, races, languages, religions, income levels, genders, disabilities, and knowledge levels.

Think Equal is a global initiative that calls for a system change in education, to end the discriminatory mindset and the cycle of violence across our world, and ensure positive life outcomes for our children. Its patrons include the late educationalist Sir Ken Robinson, actress/activist Meryl Streep, actress Susan Sarandon, and other activists who are passionate about teaching empathy in early childhood before prejudices contaminate the child's mind.

I met Think Equal's Founder, Leslee Udwin, when she was visiting Singapore in 2017. I rallied a team of professional Early Childhood Educators led by pioneer guru Dr Khoo Kim Choo to bring in the Think Equal curriculum empathy programme taught in twenty-five countries to 240,000 kids so far.

I funded SGD 10,000 for this pilot from my own pocket for one year and Leslee donated the books. The team donated their time.

Kim Choo's team did a pilot with eighteen kindergartens for one year. We taught 400 students through puppet plays, books, and interactive role plays. All principals reported kinder kids who are more empathetic and resilient against discrimination such as racism and xenophobia. The kids learned to stop using hurtful words about different races and to empathize how other kids might feel. Our success was evident when all eighteen principals reported the kids becoming kinder in the process. The teamwork was amazing and we thought that we were making a difference in early childhood development.

Think Equal's Leslee Udwin with Singapore
team led by Khoo Kim Choo

We proposed it to the Early Childhood Development Authority (ECDA) of the Singapore government for free. But

ECDA refused to adopt it. They said they'll do it themselves. No reasons were given and they were not interested in dialogue. As I probed further, ECDA said they only set standards and guidelines and are not involved in curriculums. I tried to approach the Ministry of Education's Kindergarten, but they told me their curriculum was done and they couldn't accept any additional inputs. Without adoption at system level, I have had no success here. I'll wait for the next window of opportunity. I think there'll be a time when they realize this is important. I hope it won't be too long.

How to Handle the Ups and Downs

In this chapter, I want to address how to handle disappointments and successes.

This is how I watch a football match. When my team is winning, I am prejudiced. I can only enjoy their success if I am biased. However, when my team is losing, I become objective. I don't want to suffer the feeling of loss. I can avoid the pain if I look forward to the next game and not dwell in history.

Disappointments are painful. They can wear you down or can break your heart. The more your hopes and aspirations, the more painful are the disappointments. It gets even worse if these disappointments come unexpectedly. They can also be traumatic if caused by betrayal. However, disappointments are inevitable. The more ideas you experiment with, the more disappointments you will have. Alternatively, if you have no aspirations, you may also be disappointed with your lethargy or lack of achievements.

How you handle it will determine how you reduce the pains that accompany it. Some people say failing does not make you a failure, when the words already sound the same.

I have had lots of attempts that did not succeed in the past, some are even chronicled in the previous section of this book. I don't want to remember how many times I have failed. I can't possibly win all the time.

I managed my mind by only remembering the projects that succeeded or those I still want to work on. If I have not given up yet, I don't call them failures. I call them 'work in progress'. I remember the lessons on what to avoid and how to cope with losses and avoid bad relationships, but I carry no burden of regret or bitterness in my mind. I accept that sometimes I make stupid mistakes. But I know that being happy is a choice and being unhappy is also a choice. I choose to live light-heartedly and optimistically. I avoid anything that would reduce my energy, and work with people or things who energize me.

The first time I was invited to a TV interview, I was so excited. I called all my friends and relatives to watch me that night on News Hour. All my friends and relatives were also very excited and told me they'd be watching the programme. Then, the next week, I was on TV again and I alerted them. This time they said they'll try to watch it.

It suddenly dawned on me that something unhealthy was happening inside my mind. I was enjoying fame, and this is a trap that so many people fall victim to. I started to figure it out inside my brain: My mission is to bring forth a better quality of life for the people who lack voice. Any media publicity is for generating awareness and creating legitimacy for my mission. My mission is paramount and far higher than myself. I am one of the vehicles towards the mission and I am certainly not the mission. If I confuse my mission with my personal vanity, I will become the obstacle to my mission.

My thinking became clearer, but how do I suppress my ego that keeps jumping with joy each time I am recognized by the media or awards? Initially, I had to remind myself of my mission every hour, then as I was able to suppress my small ego, I only needed to remind myself whenever it popped up again. It took continuous training, and I knew I didn't have to totally eliminate my ego. I just had to befriend it and tell myself: 'I can enjoy my vanity a little, but not too much. The mission is more important.'

When I invite someone to volunteer or partner with my missions, I invite them to walk the journey together towards a beautiful future that we both like. I am not their leader and they're not doing it for me. We are both doing it for a mutually satisfying vision. If they leave midway, I continue walking, doing what I can with people who are doing what they can, and more people will join in this shared vision.

Lessons:

We live between attachment and detachment, and we can choose when to hold and when to let go, when to be a prisoner and when to be free.

When children are young, I am attached to them. When they become independent, I let them go.

I love my wife, but I don't own her. We are together and we are free.

The mission is not me nor is it mine. I serve it well when it is shared by everyone.

If I solely own the mission, it is limited by my personal capacity and cannot scale.

If the mission is shared by everyone, it can grow abundantly without borders and limitations.

Jack with Spiritual Leaders and Yoga Masters at Rishikesh

Meditation and Yoga

Yoga is a mental and spiritual practice aimed to control and still the mind, recognizing a detached witness-consciousness untouched by the mind and mundane suffering. I was invited by Swami Chidanand Saraswati to speak at the International Yoga Festival at Parmarth Niketan Ashram, an ashram near the Beatles Ashram in Rishikesh in the foothills of the Himalayas next to the Ganges River. About 1,000 world-renowned yoga masters gather there each year.

My speech about Sanitation and Sanity centred on how to be both physically and spiritually clean. After the speech, I tried all kinds of meditations and yoga. There were halls for sitting, standing, breathing, dancing, laughing, and even sleeping yoga. I tried to meditate but my mind was like a wild horse switching from one thought to another all the time. By dinner time, I told Swamiji that I had failed in all my attempts in meditation. My mind could not focus. He told me I was already a yoga master before I came to the yoga festival. I was puzzled but he explained:

I've never met a person who focuses so deeply thinking about Toilets, Toilets, and Toilets all the time. Your continuous meditations on this one single subject send vibrations to the universe that have caused so many others to think the same. If you did not spread the messages continuously, there would not be such a sanitation movement in the world happening by itself. Yoga is not about long beard or saffron, it is about the way you live.

Then, he gave me a smile as if to say, 'Now you know.'

I started researching and found many theories that resonate with what he said. What the yogis believe is that your thoughts and feelings, including everything in your subconscious, are transmitting a particular vibration out into the universe, and it attracts others with similar energy and inspires action. This is called the law of attraction.

I think I'll just carry on being myself. Whether I am a yoga master or not, it doesn't matter.

Lessons:

I often wonder if all that has happened in my life was a series of fortunate coincidences. But these coincidences keep on happening as if someone is planning for me. I am not religious, but I am spiritual. I don't understand how the universe works but I can humbly follow the natural flow as it sends me people and resources to grow our common mission and purpose.

Perhaps, this is because I only remember things that work out and don't dwell on the ones that don't.

GOING BEYOND THE WTO

'When Heaven destroys Men, there is Sorrow;
When Men offend Men, there is Vengeance.
Against the Wrath of Heaven, there is Forgiveness;
Against the Offence of Men, there is Hatred;
If we can forgive Heaven,
Let's also forgive Men.'

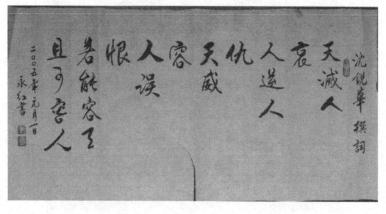

Poem composed by Jack Sim in 2004 after the Aceh tsunami

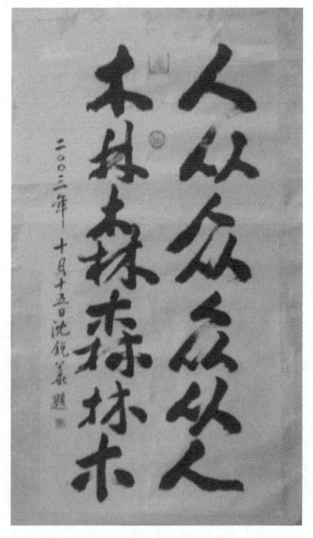

Poem by Jack Sim composed in 2003 after SARS virus outbreak

'As trees form the forest, people form society.
We're not alone, but part of each other.'

Redefining the New Billionaire

The 2017 Oxfam report says that 8 billionaires have more wealth than the lower 50 per cent of the world population combined.[37] With the slogan 'We are the 99%', the Occupy movement protested against a financial system that unfairly benefits a wealthy minority of the population. If 99 per cent of the players can't win in this game, perhaps the game's rules are wrong in the first place?

For instance, the FIFA World Cup is the biggest spectator sport with 3.5 billion viewership. It starts with 209 teams fighting for the last thirty-two qualifiers and is only won by one team. In order to find that one winner, the whole purpose of the game is to create 208 losers' nations with billions of disappointed people. Their revenue model is to make losing a form of profitable entertainment.

In a similar manner, we've created a world that regards millionaires and billionaires as winners and toilet janitors as losers. In the process, the ordinary and the lower-income folks surrender their inferiority complexes to feed the superiority of the rich people.

The 2023 Credit Suisse report showed the total wealth of the world is about USD 454 trillion, and projected that it'll be USD 629 trillion by 2027.[38] If distributed evenly, on an average, each person in the world should have more than USD 56,000 in the bank today, but the distribution of wealth is extremely uneven. In 2023, the 1 per cent richest owns half of all the money in the world, and 3.4 billion are still living in poverty earning an average of USD 5.50 a day.[39]

The world's total food production is enough to feed everyone on the planet. Paradoxically, about 40 per cent of food is wasted, while about 828 million people or 10 per cent of all humans go hungry every day.

Annually there are about USD 200 billion Official Development Assistance (ODA) donations,[40] and American individuals alone donated another USD 500 billion to charity. But where did the money go? We still have 750 million without electricity, 3.6 billion without adequate sanitation services, 2 billion without safe clean drinking water, 250 million don't go to school, 150 million homeless, according to several SDGs reports.[41]

Capitalism and democracy don't seem to be working for them when you look at the inefficient and inequitable distribution of opportunities in this current system. Extreme consumption has led to the rapid depletion of natural minerals, deforestation, the burning of forests, overexploitation of our seas, and has had an irreversible impact on the planet's climate.

Today we've reached several saturation points that are clearly unsustainable.

1. **Saturation of storage space:** The clutter in our wardrobes and storage spaces show us clear signs of over-consumption.

2. **Saturation of our body capacity:** We are breaching the maximum capacity of nutrition input that our body can accept at a healthy level.
3. **Saturation of waste to landfill:** Our throwaway lifestyle is creating unsustainable levels of waste.
4. **Saturation of the environment's capacity:** We are in ecological overshoot, currently using the earth's resources at a rate that would require 1.75 planets to sustain.
5. **Saturation of time:** Working and addiction to social media has left us with little or no time for anything else that matters in our lives.

There is a fundamental flaw in the design of our world's system that continues to perpetuate poverty, wars, territorial disputes, poor distribution of wealth and inequity, etc. Overconsumption causes uneven distribution. There is enough for everyone if we understand what is enough and start to share.

The current model is a zero-sum game that rewards 'winners' and punishes 'losers'. This 'ego system' driven by the selfish accrual of wealth is unfair: not least for the 4 billion people living at the base of the pyramid (BoP) that are excluded from the formal economy. And it's wasteful: just look at the current unemployment rates across much of Europe and elsewhere.

Relevance as Our Value System

I suggest we play a new game. In our search for a better world order, we need to design a system of recognition that motivates people to take actions with a positive impact on those around them. A billionaire should be someone who improves the lives of a billion people, or whose actions positively impact the lives of many others. We should measure our relevance as our self-worth instead of measuring our wealth. Our society cannot continue to reward unmitigated selfishness and arrogance. In our search for a better world order, we need to design a system of recognition that motivates people to take actions with a positive impact on those around them.

In fact, if relevance becomes a value system and a cultural norm, there can be tens of thousands of social billionaires because they work collaboratively to create impact, and are not chasing glory in their own names.

From 'Ego System' to Ecosystem

To facilitate an inclusive world and mobilize all resources, we need to move from this 'ego system' to an ecosystem approach. There is a long-proven sustainable model we can learn from: nature's ecosystem. The forest has no excessive hoarding mechanism. Animals eat and store food in their stomachs. They don't store wealth in banks, cupboards, refrigerators, or digital wallets. They also don't have land title deeds, even when some of them are territorial.

The forest has a governance and rebalancing system. Every organism in the forest still has to work to eat. Lazy animals die.

Put in another way, forest economics operates on a taxation system based on shit. Animals consume and give back according to their body capacity. Larger animals eat more and shit more. Smaller animals eat less and shit less. For example, big animals consume more and pay more taxes through the huge volume of excreta. A cow eats twenty-two times more food than a human, and it shits twenty-two times more than a human.

The trees shit by shedding leaves. The worms, insects, birds, fish, and bacteria shit too. All living things eat and shit and recycle their shit into nutrient resources for the growth of other living things. Herbivores eat plants while carnivores eat both herbivores and carnivores. However, genetically, herbivores are more reproductive than carnivores, and therefore, there is no overhunting of animals. In forest economics, everyone pays their fair share; humans are the only ones who cheat in their tax declarations.

Similarly, by taking an ecosystem approach in human society, we could eradicate waste, and set up an inclusive society that works for the whole population, and accepts diversity as a necessity for our survival—just like in nature's ecosystem.

It is time to reflect on what is relevant to us as people and as a society, and just as importantly what is no longer relevant so that we can find a better way of life going forward. Let's improve the state of the world in a way that's relevant to all of the people of the world.

I'm sure the new generations of young people will support this way of thinking.

Lessons:

Within our lifetime, we can collectively end global poverty and leave behind a legacy of relevance. Social entrepreneurship can succeed at an exponential scale if we create a collaborative ecosystem with policy makers, philanthropists, NGOs, media, investors, technologists, and academia towards a common mission.

Social Entrepreneurs and Biomimicry

A social entrepreneur is a person who solves social problems through market-based solutions. Social entrepreneurship emerged to fill the gaps of market failures, government failures, and charity failures that failed to lift the bottom half of the world's population out of poverty. Social entrepreneurs can speed up their impact using digital technology to create opportunities for the poor, but a joined-up approach from stakeholders is needed.

The challenge of ending poverty for the world's 4 billion poor is larger than any one entity can solve. Crucially, this task also presents a market opportunity so large that there is more than enough work for all active stakeholders to engage in. More than ever before, digital technology is making these opportunities easier to harness.

With technology now increasingly accessible—through cheap smartphones, e-payment and e-commerce systems— farmers can be connected directly to buyers, bypassing the need for a middleman, and thus reducing transaction costs and increasing independence.

These changes can have significant knock-on effects in other parts of their lives: with better prices, they can buy improved seeds to grow superior crops, which fetch higher prices. With extra income, farmers can send their kids to school or study online through free massive open online courses. They can access 'e-health' services, where doctors in cities diagnose patients in remote villages through video calls, and medications are dispensed at local village pharmacies. They can buy solar panels to pump water from boreholes, which can be filtered using affordable water tech, creating business opportunities to sell clean drinking water.

As more such trades are operated by the villagers themselves, velocity of money increases and local GDP rises, thus creating jobs and improving access to more quality-of-life products such as clothing, hairdressing and beauty products, handicrafts, micro-insurance, toilets, and more.

As social entrepreneurs, we can help facilitate this growth. But first, we must remind ourselves that we do not own the poor. They are not the tools for our survival, or our road to glory. If we truly want to support them to rise from poverty, we should muster the combined power of all stakeholders to help them.

Contrary to the belief that donating money will get the poor out of poverty, donations can do more harm than good—with a few exceptions like emergencies, disasters, refugees, etc. In fact, donations of USD 1 trillion in the last fifty years to Africa has made the lives of the poor much worse than before, resulting in 'dead aid'.[42] Freebies distort the market with the price of zero, which no businesses can compete with. Without entrepreneurs, no jobs can be created and therefore the poverty cycle continues.

We know that there are already more than 4,000 proven social business solutions that we can adaptively replicate from and integrate with. These four groups are namely Schwab Foundation of the World Economic Forum, Skoll Foundation, Ashoka, and Catalyst 2030, and they cover all the agendas under the seventeen UN Sustainable Development Goals (SDGs).

While social entrepreneurs marry markets with philanthropy to bring equity, we can further enhance our search for sustainable models by adding biomimicry to social entrepreneurship, markets, and philanthropy.

As stated on Biomimicry.org, 'biomimicry offers an empathetic, interconnected understanding of how life works and ultimately where we fit in. It is a practice that learns from and mimics the strategies used by species alive today. After billions of years of research and development, failures are fossils, and what remains hold the secret to our survival. The goal is to create products, processes, and systems—new ways of living— that solve our greatest design challenges sustainably and in solidarity with all life on earth. We can use biomimicry to not only learn from nature's wisdom, but also heal ourselves—and this planet—in the process.'[43]

We can borrow the nine basic principles of biomimicry by Janine Benyus when building our tech-driven ecosystems tailored to the low-income marketplace.

Here is my translation of the principles into practical actions:

1. **Nature runs on sunlight.** We can invest in solar energy tech to electrify off-grid communities. With energy, we can deliver water pumps, drip irrigation, Wi-Fi access, lighting, refrigeration, education, e-health, e-commerce, e-payment, and more.
2. **Nature uses only the energy it needs.** We can save energy by sharing and adaptively replicating our solutions in multiple locations, instead of inefficiently working in silos.

Through wider interconnected collaboration, we can share solutions and resources and scale up our impact without scaling up our overheads.

3. **Nature fits form to function.** We can use transparent blockchain technology to unblock any bureaucracy that hinders function, and shape public policy to blend seamlessly with social innovations.

4. **Nature recycles everything.** Beyond the mountains of solid waste daily, the next biggest waste is ideas waste. We should recycle all proven ideas and not waste the opportunity to copy from each other.

5. **Nature rewards cooperation.** Collaboration makes mission delivery cheaper, faster, better, and easier. We can achieve economies of scale through bulk buying, shared-services centres, cost engineering, common designs and common components, direct trade distribution, collective branding, media amplification, blended capital financing, and policy influence.

    These efficiencies will make those inside the collaborative ecosystem much more competitive than those outside, thus motivating them to join these open-source ecosystems as well. In this way, nobody can corner the markets and we can mitigate against the powers of extractive industries.

6. **Nature banks on diversity.** There is no such thing as a 'king of the jungle' in nature. Nature is non-hegemonic. Everything in nature has its own functions contributing to the sustainability of the whole. We should harmonize the diversity of our combined human talents, resources, and assets.

7. **Nature demands local expertise.** The current development sector is a hierarchical and condescending structure where the Organisation for Economic

Co-operation and Development (OECD) countries' donors decide what aid the poor needs. This often results in the poor getting schools with no local teachers, hospitals with no local doctors and nurses, and toilets with no maintenance. We need to engage local wisdoms, local cultures, and local talents to develop the local communities so that they can sustainably take ownership of their livelihoods and well-being after the donor's funding ends.

8. **Nature curbs excesses from within.** Many NGOs spend excessively large amounts of time and money on fundraising. I often wonder whether the beneficiaries of philanthropy are the NGOs themselves since very little is left to help the poor after their heavy overheads with layers of salaries, fundraising costs, flights, hotels, meals, conferences, and expensive consultants. Through an open collaborative ecosystem, we can mitigate the excesses from within.

9. **Nature taps the power of limits.** If each of us do only what we are good at and let the others do what they are good at within a collaborative ecosystem, we will be able to decentralize powers by building the capacity of the local stakeholders. Our objective is to maximize impact for all, instead of maximizing profits for a few. If we do not tap the power of limits, we will see more companies larger than countries and taking over political decisions to corner the markets for the billionaires with trillion dollar corporations, depriving the opportunities from the smaller participants.

The technologies available span sectors such as agritech, energy, water, sanitation, e-payment, e-commerce, logitech, edutech, housing, e-health, fintech, and smart city public policy, to name a few. We know that we do not have the trillion of dollars of foreign aid needed to deliver the seventeen Sustainable Development Goals. But if we can convert a significant portion into social business investments, and combine this with proven business models, we can solve the problem at an exponential scale and speed, and at a much lower cost than traditional methods.

On my part, I'm building a 65,000 square feet SDG Center in Singapore. We aspire BoP Hub to become a coordination centre for the base-of-pyramid marketplace, and invite all interested parties to co-create and co-design the working mechanism so that it can become a replicable, open-source model. The idea is that anyone could start similar centres around the world, allowing more social businesses to be connected with each other across borders as we strive to achieve a common goal: to improve the lives of those less fortunate than us.

This is our business call to action.

Lessons:

You can't save the world alone. Silos are inefficient. NGOs should be big-mission driven and not operate in survival mode. Through a culture of open collaboration, we can reach impact at an exponential rate. The market for the BoP is the next blue ocean.

The Biggest Blue Ocean
Marketplace in the World

President Clinton said:

'Nearly every problem has been solved by someone, somewhere. The challenge of the 21st century is to find out what works and scale it up.'

Singapore's transformation from Third World to First World relied on building self-reliance with the mantra: 'Nothing is for free.' Singapore's per capita GDP was USD 500 in 1965 when it gained independence. In 2023, Singapore's per capita GDP ranked among the top ten globally. It has now become the model of excellence in global development studies.

China copied Singapore's model of development since 1986 and lifted 800 million people out of poverty in the last forty years, according to the World Bank report in 2022. This is the largest number in human history. Their people did this through entrepreneurship, attracting investments, and job creations, instead of relying on donations.

The poverty penalty is a major global issue. Without access to the marketplace, the poor sell their commodities at low prices through middlemen and buy products at higher prices than the rest of us.

For example, they borrow money at an interest rate between 24 and 50 per cent per annum from microfinance companies. And if they have to borrow from loan sharks, the interest rates can be up to 50 per cent per month and human traffickers exploit such weaknesses of the poor when they can't pay.

Because they buy food, products, and services in small portions, they always pay a higher price than the rich. I once joined a microfinance meeting in Mexico City. One of the borrowers was a lady who bought shoes from the city to sell them to the villages. Her loans carried an interest rate of 32 per cent a year. I asked her how she could make a profit with such a high interest rate. She told me it was easy. She simply sold the shoes to the poor in the city at double the price she bought them for! This is a very inefficient marketplace and also a great business opportunity if we can make it efficient by lowering interests and direct purchase through e-commerce and e-payments, without intermediaries.

The only way to end poverty is through efficient marketplaces. These include areas such as health, education, energy, nutrition and sanitation, skills training and jobs creation, attracting investments, value-added processing of natural resources, and developing entrepreneurial talent.

Of the 8 billion people in the world, most goods and services serve only the 4 billion rich and middle class.

The other 4 billion lower-income folks are ignored by product manufacturers and service providers and excluded from our formal economy. These people are known as the Base of the

Pyramid (BoP) and they make up more than half of the human population. They also do not earn enough for a living wage.

While the developed world has stagnated in fertility growth, the BoP is now the only demographics with increase in population. The average growth rates of Africa and developing nations are currently higher than the matured economies.

For the longest time, the poor are portrayed as helpless, hopeless, and useless. Such negative images of naked, hungry, and dying kids are touted by NGOs to emotionally blackmail the general public into donating money to the NGOs. These images are a misunderstanding created by the developed world that the poor are not profitable and associating with the poor must be a loss-making endeavour.

In fact, the poor are entrepreneurial, hungry, and very hard working. The demand that they create is massive—from their purchasing power in everything from clean drinking water to solar energy, education and vocational training, motorcycles, food, toilets, housing, healthcare, mobile phones, and banking. What they need are investments, technology, opportunities, skills training, and market connectivity to increase their income and reduce their cost of borrowing.

Lesson:

The ultimate goal of the seventeen UN Sustainable Development Goals can be reached by converting the 4 billion poor into a vibrant, transparent, and efficient marketplace. The poverty crisis is an opportunity for all of us to apply market principles with a desire to bring about a fairer world.

BoP Hub

The biggest waste in the world is 'ideas waste'. We have to recycle and reuse good ideas and solutions to scale them globally. If we all knew what we all knew, we could end poverty by sharing experiences and knowledge.

I set up the BoP Hub in 2011 with an audacious goal to become a solutions clearing house to serve an ecosystem of abundance by working with social entrepreneurs and businesses to adaptively replicate proven solutions, business models, policies, and technologies from one source to as many locations as possible, powered by software.

Our vision is to provide everyone with opportunities to sustain their livelihood with dignity. By connecting partners and sharing resources, we can create a self-generating market ecosystem to attract investments, build capacity, drive demand, increase income, and create multipliers lifting the poor out of poverty.

The best way to end poverty is to help them build their capacity to help themselves. We can train them in vocational skills, teach them to do business, transfer technology to them, lend them money or invest in them to grow their businesses and make profits. We can also help them in value-added processing for higher profit margins, obtaining certification, design packaging, branding, and distribution channels for both local and export markets. As more businesses employ more people, they generate their own economy and soon their income becomes expenditure and they can afford a better quality of life like safe drinking water, housing, health, education, energy, cooking stoves, lighting, drip-irrigation, fast-moving consumer goods, logistics, transportation, nutrition, ICT communication, and even entertainment. When we unlock the spirit of enterprise and good work ethics of the people, we open pathways into prosperity.

The poor of today will become the middle-class of tomorrow. By having clean water, hygiene, and sanitation, the poor can be healthier and more productive to earn more money. With technology like e-commerce and e-payments, they can cut out many of the middlemen and get better prices for their produce by buying and selling directly.

Sixty per cent of the poor reside in Asia. The BoP Hub, with its 65,000 square feet SDG Center in Singapore can coordinate, integrate, and facilitate all BoP businesses across sectors and across geographies. Whatever lessons we learn in our successes in Asia can be shared with our counterparts in Africa, Latin America, and other parts of the world.

Currently, it takes twenty NGOs working in silos to deliver twenty different products and services through twenty different distribution channels. We can replace such inefficiencies by cutting duplications through using just one clearing house and delivery channel, saving the unnecessary cost because of duplications of overheads. Instead of start-ups, we can focus on scaling up existing proven business models found all over the world and accelerate them through established organizations as partners.

There are 450 Schwab Fellows of the World Economic Forum[44] spread across the globe covering all the seventeen UN SDGs. There are also nearly 4,000 Ashoka social innovators,[45] and another 300 Skoll Fellows.[46] These thousands of social innovators with proven solutions are listed under https://catalyst2030.net/ and can be our starting points.

By blending donations with venture capital, technology, and existing proven scalable business models, we can reduce risk, increase successes, and transform billions of dollars of charities and foreign aid into investments for the BoP marketplace.

Entrepreneurship can bring both wealth and social justice. What we need is the exponential mindset to address this prosperity challenge at an exponential scale by thinking system change instead of working in silos.

With our DNA of trust, efficiency, connectivity, stability, and our infrastructure in finance, communication, technology, and public policy, Singapore can become one of the global centres for the 4 billion new customers if we put all our genius together in alignment.

I know we can end global poverty because I've witnessed the Singapore economic miracle growing up in the 1960s to 1990s.

The BoP marketplace is certainly the next new blue ocean we must not miss. Access to the internet can lower transaction costs for the poor. Downstream processing of their primary products can value-add their income. Raw coffee beans can become roasted coffee powder with simple factories and quality control. With proper formulation, raw cocoa can be made into chocolate powder for drinks. Timber logs can become designer furniture. Overproduction of mangoes can be made into snacks and sold at higher prices. If we train the locals to create local factories with quality control and certifications, we can improve the income of the poor from say USD 2 a day to USD 6 a day and help them get out of poverty.

Through global collaboration, we can now do the same for all the people in the world.

Lessons:

Here are some of the best models to help end poverty:

1. BRAC is an international development social enterprise founded in Bangladesh serving over 100 million people living with inequality and poverty to create opportunities to realize human potential. Its social business models are worth replicating.
2. Singapore is a country that transformed itself from poverty to wealth within one generation of twenty-five years. Its public policies are an excellent model for development.
3. China lifted 800 million people out of poverty using market-based solutions and is now the second largest economy in the world. This transformation took only thirty years.

The Countdown: Death as a Motivator

When I reached the age of forty, I remember asking myself what do I want to say to myself at the end of this journey? Looking at the other houses along my street at Meyer Rd— my neighbours are way richer than I am—it'd be futile and miserable to compare myself with them. Similarly, fame and fortune are irrelevant since everyone has to die eventually. It does not matter whether people remember me after I am dead. When I am dead, it's all over and I won't know anything any more. All my vanities are nothing but unnecessary distractions. At the end of this journey, I want to say to myself, I did not waste the chance to make things better for our society.

I realized that time is the real currency of life. Money and food are merely means of sustenance, but life itself is the opportunity to do something meaningful. Instead of counting money, I count the remaining time left. On my fortieth birthday, I set a countdown clock on my phone, forecasting my expiry date on my eightieth birthday on 5 March 2037. I also put a time of expiry at 23.59, one minute before midnight. The average age of a male Singaporean is now eighty-three, but I budgeted eighty good years because the last three years might be low-quality years full of illness and frailties. I'll not be very useful to society when I have hearing loss, poor eyesight, low mobility, osteoarthritis, cancer, diabetes, depression, kidney failure, loss of memory, or dementia. Eighty years is only 29,200 days. I've already consumed 14,600 days, so I'm at half-time.

There is now an urgency to make every remaining day purposeful and meaningful. I cannot waste this precious diminishing thing called life. I want to live a useful life.

By the time this book is published, I'd probably have only 4,500 days left to live. And counting.

At first, my app showed the countdown—days, hours, minutes, and seconds. It made me very anxious when I saw the seconds moving so fast. I became calmer when it only counted the days.

It is natural for us to be afraid of death, since our will to live is strong. However, it is also clear that all our ancestors are dead and it is certain that we'll soon become ancestors too. We cannot save time in storage to use later. Time is consumed regardless of what we do or don't do. Since it is a perishable good, I need to exchange it for the highest value of exchange. I concluded that the highest value is service to humanity.

Since I had the privilege of working for free, I chose to address those agendas that nobody wanted to fund and were neglected, like sanitation and poverty alleviation through market-based solutions.

I am happy with myself, but I want to do more. I am greedy to serve, to solve difficult problems, to fight injustice, to be useful, and to see people's lives getting better. I also realized that time is more efficiently used if I can create movements that facilitate and help accelerate others who will implement them locally on the ground. I decided to be an orchestrator instead of a single instrument player.

If there is any legacy, I hope this book can help inspire you to find your own legacy. Legacy is for the people who are alive, not for the dead. Legacy is not about being remembered because when I'm gone I won't be here to greet the people at my funeral.

Lessons:

Life is short, live a fully useful life. Everyday is an opportunity to make the world a better place.

Do your duties to your family, communities, and the world at large.

Giving is a joy not to be missed.

How to Cope with Multiple Agendas Simultaneously

At any one time, I have more than a hundred agendas running concurrently. These may range from media interviews, toilet projects, poverty alleviation, teaching at various universities, mentoring students, engaging volunteers, negotiating partnerships, planning events, educational projects, start-up businesses, product designing, engineering, marketing, advocacy programmes, making films, writing books, business meetings, Zoom meetings, social media, government liaison, speaking engagements, exhibitions, foreign workers' issues, investments, fundraising, operations meetings, all in multiple organizations and companies, and a constant stream of novel ideations.

And then there are family activities—gardening, walking the dog in the evening, mahjong games, art works, travels, home improvements, driving the kids, and coffee with my wife.

The trick is not to remember anything and have all of them written down so that I simply follow the written plans on my phone's calendar and notes.

The RAM of my brain is always empty and all memories are put into the 'hard disk' of my brain that immediately recalls when triggered to engage in any topics.

After the discussion, my brain returns to an empty state and carries no burden or worries. This empty state of mind also allows White Space, which helps me stay creative and energized. When the mind is empty, it creates space for new ideas to come and occupy it.

This system helps me stay in the present at all times, while planning and schedules are all on my calendar and written notes. This way, I don't have to remember anything except when triggered, and so I can live light-heartedly without much stress while doing plenty of work through others.

Each piece of work is delegated to a leader and it is usually not me. I farm out implementation work to willing partners, passionate volunteers, and working colleagues. I do the creative work, trust building, advocacy and communication work as these areas are my forte.

I realized also that I have some other innate capabilities that help me survive. For example, I am able to conserve my energy by closing my eyes to rest anywhere, anytime. In a taxi, a bus, or a plane, I can wake up instantly when we arrive. I can also focus on any topic deeply, yet switch instantly to another topic with full focus if required. I can blend humour in between serious conversations and soften the edges of hard discussions without losing any of the key contents. Perhaps these are coping mechanisms that I developed over the years, perhaps in response to my ADHD, who knows?

However, the downside of keeping the RAM empty is that I often forget where I parked my car, where I put my eyeglasses, and other trivial things. I lost seven blackboards during my primary school days. I once forgot which building I'd parked my car in and I was already late for my next appointment. I was clueless and so I called my wife for ideas. She asked me to take a taxi to go into each of the nearby building car parks to search for it. I found it in the second building I tried. The lady taxi driver was laughing at me. She'd never done this before. And I also laughed at myself.

To save time searching for my spectacles, I bought ten pairs and scattered them all over the house so I can always find a pair nearby. I've learned to live harmoniously with my imperfect self. And I forgive myself each time I make silly mistakes.

This modus operandi allows me to continuously dream up new ideas without reaching saturation point. A calm mind is an unlimited source of energy. A playful mind is fun and creative.

No regrets, no blame, no grudges, no burden.

Just a light-hearted journey that attracts lots of like-minded people to join the meaningful movements serving humanity. I am able to simultaneously run seventy to eighty different types of projects with different people and still have time to look for new projects.

Lessons:

Live light and easy, without mental baggage.

If you have a bad memory, always tell the truth so that you never have to remember your lies or secrets.

Keep a good reputation with people. This is safer because when people like you, they normally won't make your life difficult.

When you are clueless, ask your wife for guidance.

I made this bronze sculpture of myself pooping at age three.

Be a Child

My daughter Earth said I'm like a twelve-year-old trapped inside a sixty-year-old's body. When I behave like a child, not knowing, not fearing, and always dreaming, I'm creative and I can experiment with my ideas and adapt till they become realities. I am oblivious of what others think of me and I am free from guilt, doubts, and negative thoughts.

My success comes from my innocence and when I am full of abundance.

On the contrary, whenever I'm rational, politically correct, and conforming, I develop self-doubts. I wonder if my dreams were possible, someone else would have already done it. I wonder if I've said the wrong things, if I've upset others, or if I'm the right person to do this, and I get confused when I have to worry about what others think of me. My mind creates an imposter syndrome that blocks me from my true abilities.

Adults have scarcity mindsets. That is why I decided never to grow up. I became a child again. I'm not childish but I'm childlike.

Adults are deteriorated children. I returned to a pre-deteriorated state. I became one of the children of my wife and I received her unconditional love, like our four kids. She became my sanctuary. As a child, I assumed that everyone loves me because I love everyone. I imagined that everyone would accept me for who I am because I accept them for who they are. I even believed I'd be forgiven if I made mistakes as long as there is an absence of malice.

As a childlike adult, I am not bothered by what others think of me. I can do whatever the crazy ideas I dream of, without fear of being judged, being laughed at, or being wrong. Deep inside me, I know I am a good person. Sometimes, my ideas don't work. I see it as normal. And I experiment again. Sometimes, my ideas work. I see it also as normal.

Sometimes, I make stupid mistakes. I see it as normal too. I simply laugh at how stupid I was and carry on.

Just as I empty my bowels and bladder regularly, I also don't carry any emotional baggage. I am light and easy. This is how I stay agile, simple, and humorous all the time.

Lessons:

Adults have to pretend to be correct all the time. It is too tiring to be an adult, to be defensive, to be hurt, and to be perfect.

Learn to be a child. Remember those days when you were loved by everyone as a child, forgiven when you made silly mistakes, and when you could reconcile with your playmates immediately after a fight without bearing grudges.

Imperfection is a much more comfortable lifestyle than trying to be perfect at all times.

Time. Energy. Priority

Everyone has some amount of time.

But if we measure time based on work done, time takes a very different dimension.

If you're tired or not interested in your work, you may have only one or two hours of productive time a day, because you'll do the bare minimum.

If you are enjoying your work, you may have eight hours of good work done.

If you think you are playing instead of working, you may even become energized or addicted to it and don't want to stop doing it beyond eight hours.

If you find meaning in the work you do, you may take it even further and bring others to join you.

If you outsource your mission to more and more people, you'll get unlimited time using other people's time.

Your energy level is generated by the level of fun and meaning you get from your work. The more energy you generate, both for yourself and your collaborators, the more time-equivalent things you can get done.

Life is not easy or difficult. It is fun or boring. When it is fun, you will get energized. Energy expands time because you can do more within the same time. But the biggest break is when you can mobilize others to join in a movement and give the ownership to others. It's like living multiple lifetimes within the same eighty-year lifespan.

I never planned to become Mr Toilet, but it happened by serendipity when the global media called me so. And then I got hooked when I discovered that social work is so much more fun than making money. Like the WTO and World Toilet Organization, Mr Toilet is very easy to remember and very hard to forget. I am proud of this nickname, because it gives an identity to the work that I do.

Life always arranges for me, and I merely follow the flow. Go with the flow; don't fight it, and it'll guide you to the place you want to be.

If you want to do something, don't worry about money, resources, authority, or even that you have no idea how to do it.

All you need to do is to start acting on it, and you'll learn how to succeed, as long as you persist till the end.

Lessons:

When you have more fun, you have more energy, and you have more time.

When you are aimless, time is wasted.

When you are tired, time is not productive.

When you have purpose and fun, lots of others will join your journeys.

The Horse and the Cart

Most businesses fail because the entrepreneur wants to make money instead of delivering values. Whether you are a businessman or an activist, the 'horse' and 'cart' have to be arranged correctly and not in reverse.

The horse is the purpose of the business. The cart is the process and the reward.

If you put the purpose as the 'driver' of the business, you have a logical arrangement.

If you put the reward (money) as the 'driver' of the business, you have an illogical arrangement. This is one of the major reasons why businesses fail.

Instead of the horse pulling the cart, you get the horse to push the cart and it becomes ineffective.

In fact, without solving a problem or satisfying a need, the business shouldn't exist in the first place. Everything starts with finding a problem to solve. When you convert the problem into a solution, you get paid for delivering the solution. If you are very good at the delivery, more customers will come for your services. When you enjoy serving them, your business grows and this perpetuates itself.

However, if you put profits before purpose, your business becomes an excuse to make your customer's money. This may dilute your passion to serve. It is your passion to serve that will grow your reputation. Internally, your staff needs to love their job beyond money too. If just like you, your staff only works for money, they can be footloose, and high staff turnover will weaken your business too. In short, a business needs a soul and that soul is its purpose.

So the next time you find yourself thinking about money first, you may need to focus more on how to deliver the purpose of the business first.

Lesson:

Money is not the purpose of a business. Money can be a by-product of the impact you have delivered. The purpose of making money is to be free from money so that we can do better things than just making more money.

How to Manufacture Luck

Looking back, nothing was planned. Everything just happened as opportunities arrived, and whenever I seized them. There must have been plenty of opportunities every day that I failed to see or seize.

But I've seized my fair share of them.

Here are some ways of handling opportunities:

Wait for opportunities. Imagine all kinds of potential scenarios that have not happened yet, and wait for them to happen.

Look for opportunities. Open your eyes wide and scan your surroundings, read widely, talk to people to verify your gut feelings, put two and two together and guess the potential synergy you can unlock between them.

Create opportunities. Dream up viable ideas and sell them actively to as wide an audience or relevant audiences. Do not be too afraid that others might copy your ideas. Execution is everything and people prefer to work with people passionate about their ideas. In social development, the more our ideas are copied, the bigger our impact. It doesn't matter who did it. Our objective is to see the impact happen.

Ride on existing opportunities. Join other people's ideas and help them grow their impact.

Create the environment for others to create opportunities. Be a facilitator or platform for others to launch their ideas and opportunities. Design collaborative environment. Design incentives for people to cooperate.

In any case, you feel good instantly when someone's situation improves through simple acts of kindness.

Here are some factors that increase your luck:

- Reliable service excellence
- Honesty in your dealings
- Humility to let others shine
- Be caring and selfless
- Empathy
- Convert gut feelings into solutions
- Patience for right timing
- Seize windows of opportunities as they appear
- Locate yourself at places with high density of serendipity
- Large media and digital presence

Lesson:

Opportunities are around you every day, but they remain invisible if you are unable to capture them. Your strengths to harvest opportunities depend on your competence to identify them, your widespread reputation, and the ripple effect of your kindness.

The Amazing Power of Pull Strategies

In Hollywood, they have a common saying: 'Don't call us, we'll call you.' This dismissive way of rejection contains a valuable and useful philosophy: It is better for people to call me than I call them. If I call them, I am not certain that they're enthusiastic potential partners and chances that I'll be rejected are high. But if they call me, they've already pre-qualified themselves as enthusiastic potential partners and I can choose to accept or reject them. 'Pull Strategy' is certainly more efficient than the 'Push strategy'. So, I focused on making myself a media darling simply by telling stories in the global media, and a magnet for potentially interested partners to call me. The global media increases the credibility and visibility of the World Toilet Organization and our messages at zero costs.

Here are some secrets to pull in media:

1. Almost all journalists reporting on social issues are activists at heart. They want to help amplify social issues and call for actions. They also want their editors to accept their reports and give them big columns or

full pages or multiple pages of coverage if possible. My job is to help the journalists succeed in making their editors happy, and I try being the newsmaker who their readers or listeners love to read about or listen to. To do that, my story has to be relevant to the current context and angle important to that place and time and audience. My daily job is to read up constantly about the 360 degrees environment so that I keep an updated awareness of what to say and what not to say. My mission is to mobilize toilets and sanitation awareness through the media with my newsworthy stories. It is a win-win direct partnership with every journalist, and indirect partnership with their editors who I normally do not have the privilege to meet.

2. 'Public Relation Value' is the ROI calculation for editorial exposure. It's calculated by multiplying the advertising cost of an ad piece of the same size in the same publication, multiplied by a factor of three. Viewers recognize a paid advertisement as a biased angle, and they place confidence in the reports from favoured media personalities at a much higher level. This makes the WTO very attractive for partnerships with corporations wanting to increase their ESG impact and values.

3. Due to limited airtime, journalists and their editors value newsmakers who are concise and sharp in responding to questions. I speak at a pace very suitable for the media. I speak with soundbites, which provide caustic pungency or appropriateness critical in getting the message through with big impact. A Dog-Bite-Man story will not sell, but a Man-Bite-Dog story will have huge viral potential.

4. The editor runs the story through a computer check and if the story is not fresh or new, he may not publish it. I've been telling the sanitation and toilet stories for the last twenty-seven years and each time it is a fresh story with new context and current framing.

5. People asked me for the essence of storytelling and how a story can remain fresh for three decades. I told them that love songs were sung for thousands of years and there are still new love songs today, sung to huge growing audiences. The stories need the storytellers who sing from their heart connecting the audiences with a voice of persuasion that touches the hearts of everyone each time. This is not a mechanical process. It is an emotional process. I have been telling Julie and my children 'I love you' multiple times a day for decades, and each time, they feel the love because it comes from the heart. You can't fake love.

I applied the same Pull philosophy in my earlier commercial businesses too. I picked the businesses by identifying an existing problem, which meant I didn't have to create the demand. I only had to be better than the current suppliers and enhance market efficiencies.

In the bricks business, it was obvious that the booming construction industry needed lots of bricks. There was no need to push my products. I pulled the customers to me.

The Australian International School was formed because there was no Australian school curriculum available in Singapore. All I needed was to supply the balm to soothe the pain and pull them to my school.

The roof tiles business was to replace an inferior product of concrete roof tiles with a superior product of clay roof tiles.

The real estate development business opportunities were caused by the fact that large real estate developers like City Development and Far East Organization were not interested in developing small plots of land thus creating a niche vacuum for me.

In short, if an entrepreneur discovers a huge unsolved problem, he has discovered a goldmine of opportunity. All he has to do is to organize the talents, money and implementers to move ideas to reality. The key success factor is to believe it can be done and to hang in there until it is successful.

Lessons:

If you knock on someone's door, you are likely to get rejected. If they knock on your door, all you have to do is to accept them if you like them.

Push strategy tends to be expensive with a low success rate. You do not know who likes you and they do not identify themselves. You need to do much research to prequalify your target.

Pull strategy works when your stories are appealing and they are everywhere. You do not know who likes you, so you let them choose you and when they call you, they've identified themselves. You do not need to research nor prequalify your targets, they reveal themselves to you.

Lovers and Prostitutes

Each day, we wake up and spend most of our waking hours working. There are people who enjoy their work passionately, and there are people who do it merely as a meal ticket. There are also people who hate their jobs but continue to work under stress.

There are many shades of grey but for ease of understanding, I'd now generalize them into two breeds of workers at the two extreme ends of the spectrum.

The Prostitute

The prostitute sells their body for money. Their work environment is unsafe. Their bosses are pimps who exploit them, make money from their labour, and pay them little. Their colleagues snatch their customers. Their hygiene factors at work are risky. And their self-images are low or without dignity. They even have to fake enjoyment to please the boss and customers. They live in a state of tolerance. They feel unloved. They wonder if there is a better way to earn a living.

Now when we transfer this analogy into the office, we're surprised there are plenty of similarities. There are plenty of people who drag themselves to work each morning. They hate their work but sell their labour to the company for eight or more hours. They fear their colleagues who try to claim credit for their work, fake results, and suck up to the bosses. When the workplace is toxic, people play office politics, trust is gone, rules are heavy, and their energy is draining every day. In turn, this affects both the mental and physical health of themselves and those around them.

You will be amazed how many prostitutes are at your workplace. Many suffer burnout syndrome eventually. They wonder if there is a better way to make a living.

The Lover

Fortunately, there is another breed of workers who love their work and are deeply immersed in the process. They wake up every day full of zest and purpose to go to work. Their performance uplifts everyone's morale.

Lovers are enthusiastic, creative, and work is play to them.

A lover is an unstoppable force of nature in building up the momentum, and they encourage others to become lovers too. The workplace is energized and everyone wants to work where there are lots of lovers. The performance results are in a state of ecstasy constantly.

So, the question is are you a lover or a prostitute?

If you discover you're a prostitute, it's best to leave the job and change your life.

The good news is when prostitutes discover their true love, they become a lover. While a prostitute might fake enjoyment at work, they can be truly enjoying the togetherness with their partners outside of work. Of course, not everyone has the privilege to leave their job, or have no choice but to work in a job they hate due to financial commitments. Some may also dislike the job at a lower degree, and are able to tolerate it. It is not binary.

So, the real question is what do you really love to do? What would give you a deep sense of meaning and purpose? Your choices are personal and only you can define your purpose. The key is to know that you can choose.

All the world loves a lover.

The cons of being a prostitute outweigh the pros.

Be a lover and live the life you have always wanted to live.

Lessons:

Life is short and we need to love what we are doing every day to live a quality life.

Unless you are working under duress, you should not feel trapped inside a job. Leave toxic environments because they are bad for mental and physical well-being. Learn new skills and open up your horizon.

My Hopes for the Future

I've experienced a blissful uninhibited childhood, a confusing teenage era, a transition to adulthood full of mistakes, a successful career, survived a bout of depression at midlife during the Asian Financial Crisis, the joy of bringing up four lovely kids, a purposeful journey of service, and continuous romance with Julie.

Life is simply a series of experiences to cherish. Each phase of life follows natural laws and each has its own time and place. I cannot deny the natural process of life. My kids are now of marriageable age. Soon they'll set up their own families and have their own homes. Julie and I will experience the empty nest syndrome, which can be emotionally challenging for her if I am not around always.

Instead of waiting for possible problems to start, I can turn it into an opportunity to romance my wife, a chance to spend time with just the two of us again. We can repurpose our time and strengthen our intimacy as we begin our new chapter in life. We have started going on short honeymoon trips again. The ultimate Royal Caribbean Sea cruise trip is 274 days in sixty-plus countries. There is no point saving too much money for when you are old. It's better to spend it while you are still physically able to travel and enjoy the world at a leisurely pace.

I have to do what my body and mind tell me to do at each stage of the journey. In another ten years, I might be frail and unable to work with vigour and mobility. I have to learn to synchronize myself with the universe and surrender gracefully to the counsel of age.

Just as others plan their last will, I have to allocate the remaining time to a bucket list:

1. **World Toilet Organization**

   We've achieved a quarter century and the world toilet movement now has a life of its own. However, in the myriad of agendas and priorities, the Sanitation Agenda constantly runs the risk of being drowned by Water and other agendas as other priorities like Climate Change overwhelm every other agenda. On the media side, sanitation competes against everything else for visibility. This includes football, news, movies, games, music, and Kim Kardashian's new dress. For WTO 2.0, the World Toilet Organization needs to transform itself from a founder-led global movement to a strong institution with structure and self-sustaining financial models to facilitate the mission in a more organized manner.

   The next generation might not be able to work for free. WTO needs to build revenue models to help it become financially strong. I have to find a team of passionate leaders and let them take over. Technology is now very advanced, and we can unify all sanitation efforts in all countries, and facilitate this global sanitation movement exponentially. A donor has sent us a consultant to help us design new structures and revenue models so as to allow me to invite a new chairman and patrons. I can continue to be the storyteller and evangelist, but not be involved in management any more. A new Executive Director will take over that role. In Toilet language, I am going to 'let go'.

2. **BoP Hub**

Ending global poverty for the 4 billion poor is a much larger mission than bringing toilets for 2.6 billion people or safely managed sanitation to 4.5 billion people. Sanitation is only one of the many services and needs of the poor. With the experience gained from orchestrating multiple stakeholders in sanitation, the same methodology can be applied to off-grid energy, non-sewered sanitation, offline education, water, housing, healthcare, agritech, fintech, investments, jobs creation, transportation, infocomm, etc. by weaving them into an efficient self-generating digital marketplace beyond the charity buying models.

Besides our Board members, we need to partner with technology leaders. The challenge is huge but necessary to bring equity and social justice to all people. We cannot bear to see fellow humans live without the basic needs and decency. Our ethos as a servant to facilitate the success of others will serve our common mission well. Our role is to connect the energies of diverse entities and orchestrate them into ecosystems that can unlock their synergies and produce natural prosperity at exponential scale.

3. **Detachment from Duties**

Eventually, the journey will come to an end and I'll not be able to function productively even if I want to.

Like gangsters at the end of the street waiting to beat me up, there will be many maladies awaiting me as my body surrenders to them. Their names are cancer, strokes, heart diseases, pneumonia, kidney failure, urinary tract infections, and lung diseases, and they can even call up reinforcement to kill me one way or another with a combination of multiple failures of minor and major malfunctions.

I need to gracefully surrender the more youthful pace of life and move into the final phase of life based on the budgeted eighty years of useful life. Beyond that, it is bonus time.

I appreciate my journey immensely. I just want to make things better and inevitably focus on the missing gaps instead of the praises. I appreciate the well-managed Singapore where I've had the privilege to spend my life. I appreciate the opportunities to have seen the world, having travelled almost seventy countries, and savour the amazing range of cultures, the way they survive, their love for families, their passion for life, and how they remember their loved ones.

I think I've done my fair share of service to humanity. It is always possible to do more, but there is always an end point for everything. Having lived an unplanned life, I want the end point to be planned a bit more. I don't want to die in the office.

I believe that the ultimate freedom is to owe the world nothing, to want nothing, and to be free from expectations. The last phase of life has to be personal and an inwards journey. I have been seeing things widely. Now I want to see things more deeply. I want to be a child again. Perhaps, I can become the artist that I've always wanted to be since childhood, and perhaps this can be done by learning AI generated images, songs, stories, movie scripts, etc.

At or near the final moment, I'd like to tell myself I have not wasted the opportunity of every moment to live a life full of abundance. I've allocated these proportionately towards a balanced life. I'd congratulate myself for having met Julie, Faith, Truth, Worth, and Earth, and my parents, my brother, William, and my sister, Sylvia, and all the people I've met plus all those who I've not met but connected with indirectly through these journeys.

While I've tried to plan my life, life planned it better than me. I am thankful for the privilege to serve, the chance to love, and the opportunity to live a useful life. Most of all, it was fun.

Mr Toilet's Cheat Sheet

Here is a list of life hacks I hope you will take away from this book.

1. If you have a raw idea, start working on it and you will learn how to do it by doing it.
2. Fall in love with your mission; the deeper your love, the faster you'll learn.
3. The world has an oversupply of followers, and a shortage of leaders. If you lead, they'll follow you.
4. Everyone is trustworthy for some things but not for all things. They are trustworthy in things that they're motivated and competent in.
5. Most people are creative, unless someone kills it.
6. Everyone is seeking benefits; mutual exploitation is collaboration.
7. Everyone is selfish. Collective selfishness is selflessness.
8. You can achieve everything, as long as you can get others to do it passionately.
9. If you discover a problem, you discover an opportunity. The bigger the problem, the bigger the opportunity. Choose the ones you love to solve.
10. Imagine all the talents and resources waiting to partner with you. All you have to do is to invite them.

11. Life is an opportunity to do something marvellous before your time limit is up. Don't waste your precious time.
12. If you take the risk, it may or may not happen. If you don't take the risk, it'll never happen.
13. A No Entry sign says Find Next Entry.
14. Our body is an efficient ecosystem. Make our society function like our body, with every organ in collaboration.
15. We must be always moral and ethical. But not always legal. We need to break some rules to change the system.
16. If someone calls you a misfit, help them for they are a conformist.
17. Avoid people who reduce your energy. Work with people who increase your energy.
18. Do not moralize the problem, solve the problem.
19. If a politician is 90 per cent corrupt, use the last 10 per cent of goodness in him.
20. Love everyone by default, and it'll be easier for them to love you back.
21. Assume everyone loves you, but don't try to find out if that is true.
22. There is nothing wrong with you, don't waste time doubting yourself.
23. You only live once, live meaningfully.

Acknowledgements

This book is an accumulation of all the thoughts from the past and present.

When Penguin Random House asked me to write this book, I did not have the experience to do such a long project.

It started as a collection of random thoughts, which I tried to arrange into a flow.

I want to thank Cassandra Chia and Surina Jain for their professional guidance in editing this book.

I am grateful to my friends Cheryl Tang, Alec Morton, and Pratibimb Dwivedi for putting in so many hours lovingly correcting and editing my early drafts.

I'd also like to thank all the people who helped me along my journey of life. Here are their names: HRH King Willem-Alexander, George Yeo, Tommy Koh, ESM Goh Chok Tong, President Tharman Shanmugaratnam, President Bill Clinton, Lee Poh Wah, Klaus Schwab, Hilde Schwab, Francois Bonnici, Goy Phumtim, Bill Drayton, Jeroo Billimoria, Kevin Teo, Naina Batra, Koh Poh Chai, Chua Hung Meng, Chan Chee Kong, L C Khong, Victor Lim, Sarika Saluja, Calvin Chu, Sandeep Khanna, Delph Mak, Adam Murad Mokhtee, Nielsen, Trudi Bishop, Royce Wee, William Sim, Tan Tong Cheng, Yap Swee Cheng, Bai Lin, Mechai Viravaidya, Ho Chee Kit, Tan Puay Hoon, Emerson Hee, Lita Nithinayanda, Tony Tan, Artur Wala,

Nick Elliot, Dilip Shankar, Edward Liew, Kumar Dilip, Ravi Bhatnagar, Patty O'Hare, H.H. Swami Chidanand Saraswati, Suleiman Adamu, Jan Kenneth Eliasson, Lily Zepeda, Tchavdar Georgiev, Jessic Yu, Roshan Shrestha, Doulaye Kone, Neeta Pokhrel, K Shanmugam, Vanu Gopalan Menon, Bilahari Kausikan, Borg Tsien Tham, Karen Tan, Kenzo Hiroki, Dave Holland, Tan Soo Sam, Jack Neo, Willie Cheng, Laurence Lien, Tay Kheng Soon, and so many more who came and walk along this beautiful journey.

I hope I've done justice to their effort and you can find this book useful for your journeys as well.

All royalties for this book will be donated to the World Toilet Organization, a registered charity in Singapore.

If you'd like to engage me as a speaker, please contact me at jacksim@worldtoilet.org.

Thank you for your support.

Appendix

Jack's Formal Courses

1. Ashoka ASPIRe Program @Societal Thinking India (3 years).
2. Harvard Business School: Special Perspectives in Nonprofit Management (1 week).
3. Harvard Kennedy School: Impact Measurement (1 week).
4. Harvard Kennedy School: Governance for Nonprofit (1 week).
5. ExO Works: Exponential Organization's Coaching (5 weeks).
6. University of Life Science, Oslo: Sustainable Sanitation Technology (1 week).
7. Karolinska University, Sweden: Hygiene and Preventive Health (1 week).
8. Linköping University, Sweden: Ecological Sanitation (1 week).
9. Uppsala University, Sweden: Nutrients Recycling and Agriculture (1 week).
10. Tata University, Bangalore, India: Sanitation Crisis (1 week).
11. Singapore Institute of Surveyors and Valuers: Professional Diploma in Real Estate Marketing (4 years).

12. Singapore Institute of Surveyors and Valuers: Certified Real Estate Agent (6 months).
13. National Productivity Board, Singapore: Diploma in Business Administration (18 months).
14. University of Strathclyde, Glasgow, UK: Master's in International Marketing (10 years but received a Post Graduate Diploma).
15. Vocational and Industrial Training Board, Singapore: Hotel and Catering Certificate (18 months).
16. The Singapore Manual & Mercantile and Workers' Union: Union Leadership (1 week).
17. Samaritans of Singapore: Listening and Emotional Resilience (9 months).

Endnotes

1   https://www.parliament.uk/globalassets/documents/post/pn190.pdf

2   https://www.theguardian.com/society/2007/jan/19/health.medicineandhealth3

3   https://www.who.int/news-room/fact-sheets/detail/diarrhoeal-disease#:~:text=It%20is%20both%20preventable%20and,childhood%20diarrhoeal%20disease%20every%20year

4   https://www.lixil.com/en/impact/sanitation/pdf/white_paper_en_cc_2016.pdf

5   https://blogs.worldbank.org/developmenttalk/half-global-population-lives-less-us685-person-day

6   https://www.straitstimes.com/singapore/nearly-two-thirds-of-singaporeans-find-public-toilets-are-as-dirty-as-in-2020-study

7   https://www.toiletboard.org/investing-in-sanitation-for-a-healthier-tomorrow/

8   https://www.mse.gov.sg/resource-room/category/2021-09-13-written-reply-to-pq-on-nea-toilet-improvement-programme/
https://www.channelnewsasia.com/commentary/singapore-cleanliness-tray-return-public-toilets-fines-3425521#:~:text=Since%20the%20first%20Keep%20Public,Shouldn't%20Be%20Scary%20video

9   https://www.straitstimes.com/singapore/politics/2024-to-
    be-the-year-of-public-hygiene-with-targeted-measures-
    to-improve-cleanliness

10 https://www.economist.com/britain/2023/08/10/in-
    defence-of-britains-public-toilets
        https://theweek.com/public-sector/960428/loos-lose-
    the-demise-of-public-toilets-in-the-uk

11 https://www.straitstimes.com/singapore/teh-cheang-wan-
    case-no-way-a-minister-can-avoid-investigations

12 https://gfmag.com/data/worlds-richest-and-poorest-
    countries/

13 https://www.theguardian.com/global-development/2012/
    feb/03/liberia-sanitation-johnson-sirleaf-toilets

14 https://www.theguardian.com/global-development/2016/
    sep/09/thirst-for-saving-lives-united-nations-
    water-man-jan-eliasson-deputy-secretary-
    general#:~:text=%E2%80%9CIt's%20an%20
    investment.,People%20go%20to%20work.

15 https://www.youtube.com/watch?v=vZgkUon3XlE

16 https://worldpopulationreview.com/country-rankings/
    hindu-countries

17 https://www.linkedin.com/pulse/swachh-bharat-abhiyan-
    from-55-open-defecation-110-prabakar-

18 https://www.telegraph.co.uk/global-health/climate-and-
    people/indias-sewer-workers-risk-snakes-toxic-gases/

19 http://www.swachhtakipehel.com/images/program-
    reports/HWTC-Annual-Report-Year4.pdf

20 https://www.youtube.com/watch?v=jQCqNop3CIg

21 https://www.fdiintelligence.com/content/news/brazils-
    sanitation-bill-to-unlock-private-investment-78399

22 https://www.bnamericas.com/en/analysis/the-upcoming-
    privatizations-concessions-and-ppps-in-brazils-
    sanitation-sector

23 https://content.time.com/time/specials/packages/
   article/0,28804,1841778_1841781_1841822,00.html
24 https://www.susana.org/en/knowledge-hub/projects/
   database/details/202#
25 https://www.theguardian.com/lifeandstyle/
   shortcuts/2018/mar/21/why-women-face-longer-
   toilet-queues-and-how-we-can-achieve-potty-
   parity#:~:text=In%20fact%2C%20the%20queues%20
   are,women%2C%2040%20seconds%20for%20men
26 https://news.un.org/en/story/2014/11/484032
27 https://vimeo.com/34792993
28 https://vimeo.com/ondemand/mrtoilettheworlds2man
29 https://med.stanford.edu/news/all-news/2020/04/smart-
   toilet-monitors-for-signs-of-disease
30 https://www.ncbi.nlm.nih.gov/pmc/articles/
   PMC10311987/
        https://www.zdnet.com/home-and-office/smart-home/
   ces-2023-sees-the-launch-of-two-smart-toilet-sensors/
31 https://www.businesstimes.com.sg/startups-tech/startups/
   gut-biome-startup-amili-raises-us105m-series-round-led-
   vulcan-capital
32 https://sato.lixil.com/
33 https://avpn.asia/
34 https://www.straitstimes.com/singapore/10-quotes-from-
   mr-lee-kuan-yews-awesome-1977-speech-in-parliament
35 'Fortifying migrant workers in Singapore', https://www.
   youtube.com/watch?v=kelrvGcFa5c
36 https://en.wikipedia.org/wiki/Singaporeans#:~:
   text=Singaporeans%20with%20Chinese%20ancestry%
   20make,excluding%20persons%20holding%20
   Permanent%20Residency).
37 https://www.theguardian.com/global-development/2017/
   jan/16/worlds-eight-richest-people-have-same-wealth-

as-poorest-50#:~:text=The%20world%27s%20eight%20
richest%20billionaires,and%20dangerous%20concentrati-
on%20of%20wealth

38   https://www.investopedia.com/global-wealth-is-
projected-to-rise-38-by-2027-7643537#:~:text=By%20
2027%2C%20global%20wealth%20will,of%202.8%25%20
or%20%2411.3%20trillion

39   https://www.oxfam.org/en/press-releases/mega-rich-
recoup-covid-losses-record-time-yet-billions-will-live-
poverty-least

40   https://www.wfpusa.org/articles/why-americans-donate-
what-motivates-people-to-give-and-what-causes-do-
they-give-to/
     https://devinit.org/resources/aid-2022-key-facts-
official-development-assistance-oda-aid/

41   https://www.npr.org/2023/03/22/1165464857/billions-
of-people-lack-access-to-clean-drinking-water-u-
n-report-finds#:~:text=Around%202%20billion%20
people%20around,Water%20Development%20Report%20
released%20Wednesday.
     https://unstats.un.org/sdgs/report/2023/

42   https://www.forbes.com/2009/04/07/summary-dead-aid-
opinions-business-visionaries-moyo.html

43   www.biomimicry.org

44   I am a Fellow here: https://www.schwabfound.org/

45   I am a Fellow here: https://www.ashoka.org/en-sg

46   https://skoll.org/